WESTWARD THE WAY

This book

has been published to commemorate

the one hundred and fiftieth anniversary

of the

Louisiana Purchase

The Last of the Buffalo
By Albert Bierstadt

WESTWARD THE WAY

The character and development

of the Louisiana Territory

as seen by artists and writers

of the nineteenth century

Edited by

PERRY T. RATHBONE

CITY ART MUSEUM OF ST. LOUIS

in collaboration with the

WALKER ART CENTER, MINNEAPOLIS

Contents

INTRODUCTION 7
by Perry T. Rathbone

ACKNOWLEDGMENT 10

HISTORY AND CHARACTER
OF THE LOUISIANA TERRITORY 13
by Frederick E. Voelker

ILLUSTRATIONS AND COMMENTARY 32
Selected by Catherine Filsinger and
William N. Eisendrath, Jr.

ESSAYS
by Perry T. Rathbone

THE LAND: RIVER, PLAIN AND MOUNTAIN 29
THE INDIAN 71
THE BIRDS AND ANIMALS 127
THE WHITE MAN 165
THE SETTLEMENTS:
FORTS, TOWNS AND CITIES 213
WESTWARD BY LAND AND BY WATER 247

LENDERS 259

CATALOGUE 261

BIOGRAPHIES OF THE ARTISTS 273

COLOR PLATES

ALBERT BIERSTADT, *The Last of the Buffalo* frontispiece

SETH EASTMAN, *Lacrosse Playing Among the Sioux Indians* facing 105

CHARLES WIMAR, *The Buffalo Dance* facing 121

FRANCES F. PALMER, *The Rocky Mountains. Emigrants Crossing the Plains* between 200-201

Introduction

"WE HAVE LIVED long, but this is the noblest work of our lives." Robert Livingstone, American Minister to France thus addressed himself to James Monroe, special envoy of President Jefferson, the two statesmen having just purchased Louisiana on behalf of the United States. The place was Paris; the date, May 2, 1803. The following year on March 9, Major Amos Stoddard of the United States Army crossed the Mississippi in a rowboat and the next day hoisted the American flag in St. Louis. This simple ceremony symbolized a political event that was to change the course of modern history. The United States had assumed final possession of its new domain, a vast area which doubled the size of the young Republic virtually overnight.

This book, and the exhibition on which it is based, has been assembled to honor the great event—that "noblest work" which took place one hundred and fifty years ago—the Louisiana Purchase.

Westward the Way, both the exhibition and the book, is an undertaking of the City Art Museum of St. Louis with the added sponsorship of the Walker Art Center of Minneapolis. It is peculiarly fitting that St. Louis and Minneapolis should join hands to celebrate this occasion. For together these two very different cities of the Mississippi signify an important aspect of the cultural development of the Louisiana Territory. St. Louis, on the one hand, with a history reaching back nearly two hundred years, remains emblematic of the culture and traditions which adhered to Louisiana before the Purchase and which were inherited with it—that of the old French and the fur trade—while Minneapolis, on the other hand, typifies the development that came with the purely American settlement of the region after the period of exploration.

The history of the United States has been in large part the history of the westward migration of the American people from the Atlantic to the Pacific. Various historical factors determined this development, but of them all the annexation of Louisiana gave the drive to the West by far its greatest impulse. With the peace that ensued following the War of 1812, the migratory movement gathered momentum like a great wave which reached its climax in the middle of the nineteenth century, and in its magnitude and swiftness created a chapter in man's history without parallel. The emigrants entered a country of which Americans had no detailed knowledge and of which Europeans were only dimly conscious. But as the wilderness was brought under control interest in the hinterland of America grew and grew. With each passing decade of the nineteenth century the frontier assumed a deeper significance and the evidence of the experience of the West, its look, its life and its character, became an increasing concern of artist and writer.

What was the character of the huge and almost unknown country beyond the Mississippi, its plains and deserts, its woodlands, mountains and waterways; what were the Indians really like who enjoyed its freedom and its bounty unchecked except by tribal rivalries; what were the birds and beasts that inhabited it; who were the pioneers—the frontiersmen, the voyageurs and the mountain men, the explorers and adventurers, the emigrants and the settlers; how did the fortified outposts, the growing settlements, young towns and cities look to these people in the van of civilization; and finally what means of transportation did they enjoy as the century advanced? These questions represent the chapters of the story we have attempted to tell in *Westward the Way*.

Fortunately the nineteenth century, as it ran its course, provided abundant documentation of itself in picture and word. Upon these we have relied in making this book. As Francis Henry Taylor has pointed out, the modern thirst for knowledge has brought about a new type of scholarship, consisting of the selection and interpretation of pictures as a visual-literary form. *Westward the Way* is an example of this new approach. In it art, literature and social history are combined.

The earliest penetrations of the Louisiana Territory as an American possession, and the many excursions and independent wanderings of certain hardy adventurers that followed, yielded written accounts of the new land of absorbing interest and fascination. As the wilderness was opened, settlements established and the migratory flood rose to its high tide, the demand for books about the West increased in similar proportion. The writers of the day were alert to the need, in Europe as well as America, and volume after volume poured from the presses. A number of these have become classics known to everyone; far more are almost totally forgotten or known only to the specialist today. Likewise the artist, within two decades of the Purchase commenced his work of recording the life and landscape of the new land in almost all its major aspects. As one writer put it, he "doubted if the brush had ever followed so hard on the rifle." As in the case of the printed word, some of these works are American classics, others are almost unknown; some are published here for the first time.

The life of the old West was born, flourished and died within such a relatively short span of years that while its larger aspects are well remembered, much of its once familiar detail is forgotten. The subject matter of many of the pictures included here would not readily explain itself to the average person. In consequence, an effort has been made to explain the subject where necessary, and augment the significance of all the pictures, by carefully selected quotations from the writers of the period, and to present them as a text to each illustration. So diligent and resourceful has this research been—no less than one hundred books have been read and reread—that in many cases the picture would appear to have been painted to illustrate the passage chosen or the excerpt written to describe the picture. Sometimes, as in the case of Bodmer and Catlin, it has been possible to employ the very picture that was made to illustrate the text. Thus the great story of the opening of the West is told verbally and graphically by many of the gifted men and women who experienced it and felt deeply about it, and who deserve to be better known by our generation which looks upon this chapter of our past with increasing nostalgia.

Neither exhibition nor book lays claim to completeness. Many works that we had ardently hoped to include lay beyond our reach for one reason or another. Moreover, the pictorial record of the West is so large that even all the most significant works could not be embraced by one exhibition or one book. Yet the pictures here assembled constitute a representative cross-section. The touchstone of selection had several sides: excellence as works of art, rarity and unfamiliarity, diversification and comprehensiveness. Thus the collection includes some of the masterpieces by American artists of the nineteenth century as well as works hitherto unknown or obscure and which possess the added fascination of rarity or early date. Comprehensiveness demanded the inclusion of the lithographic prints of some of the later topographic artists whose original drawings, alas, have disappeared.

A conscientious effort was made to include only those pictorial records that deal with the life and the land of the Louisiana Territory during the period of its exploration, settlement and development—roughly one hundred years—until the closing of the last frontier in the 'nineties.

As background for the story told by the artists and writers of the day, Frederick E. Voelker has written an informative introductory essay on the history and character of the Louisiana Territory, and the editor has written a brief foreword on the artistic activity represented in each of the six chapters of the book. A catalogue of the pictures and short biographies of all the known artists represented are also included.

Perry T. Rathbone

Acknowledgment

The preparation of *Westward the Way* has incurred a debt to many people. Those who have been closest to the project from the beginning are members of the staff of the City Art Museum. To William N. Eisendrath, Jr. I am deeply grateful for his invaluable assistance in organizing the exhibition and preparing the contents of this book for the press. Upon him and Miss Catherine Filsinger fell the task of reading a large part of the literature of the West in searching for the passages quoted in the following pages. To Miss Filsinger I am also grateful for the critical reading not only of my manuscript but that of Mr. Voelker as well. I also wish to thank my colleagues, Mrs. Louis Horton for handling many details of the exhibition; Miss Agnes Gray for her help in preparing the book for the press; and Miss Vivian Fullerton and Miss Sheila Murphy for typing the manuscript.

On behalf of the Trustees of the City Art Museum of St. Louis and the Walker Art Center, Minneapolis, I wish to express my gratitude to all the private collectors and museums who have so generously made loans to the exhibition and have given permission to reproduce works of art in their possession.

To Mr. Frederick E. Voelker I am grateful for his help in identifying the subject matter of many of the pictures, for valuable suggestions and for his introductory essay. For unfailing help and courtesy in securing loans and providing information, I should like to record my thanks to Mr. W. F. Davidson of M. Knoedler and Company, New York, as well as to the following librarians for their patience and generous assistance: Mrs. Henry W. Howell Jr. of the Frick Art Reference Library, New York; Mr. Russell F. Barnes of the James Jerome Hill Reference Library, St. Paul; Mr. Clarence Miller of the Mercantile Library, St. Louis and Miss Mildred Boatman, head of the Reference Department of the St. Louis Public Library. My thanks are also due to the staffs of the following institutions: the Minnesota Historical Society, especially Miss Bertha Heilbron and Mr. Eugene D. Becker; the Chicago Historical Society and its assistant director, Mr. H. Maxson Holloway; and the Missouri Historical Society, St. Louis, especially its Curator, Miss Marjory Douglas, Mrs. Frances Biese and Miss Barbara Kell; and to Mr. John Ewers of the Smithsonian Institution, Washington, D.C.

In preparing this book the Museum has incurred the debt of the Travelers Insurance Company for generously presenting the plates of the Currier and Ives lithograph; and of the McGraw Hill Publishing Company for permission to reproduce the color engravings of the following paintings: *The Last of the Buffalo* by Bierstadt, *Lacrosse Playing Among the Sioux* by Eastman and the *Buffalo Dance* by Wimar.

Finally, I should like to express my indebtedness to those scholars whose original research in the art of the West has been relied upon repeatedly in preparing this book. Chief amongst these are the following: David I. Bushnell, Bernard DeVoto, John Francis McDermott, Robert Taft and Charles van Ravenswaay.

P. T. R.

The History and Character of the Louisiana Territory

By Frederick E. Voelker

IN THE MIDDLE of the seventeenth century a vast, unexplored wilderness lay at the heart of the land mass that became the United States. A century or more before, Spanish adventurers had nibbled at its southern and eastern edges; and in the intervening hundred years that was all any explorer did; but in 1682 one of them, La Salle, descending the Mississippi, claimed and named the unknown territory "Louisiana" for his king, Louis XIV of France. Hence the name Louisiana designating a mid-continental region, undefined and practically unknown, acquired a nebulous political meaning.

Gradually, a decade or two after 1700, French enterprise worked northward, from the newly-established settlement of New Orleans, and out upon the waters of the lower Missouri, reaching westward for Rocky Mountain fur and southwestward for Spanish gold, and even thinking about the Pacific Ocean. The northern reaches of Louisiana, too, were being penetrated by French explorers from Canada and some knowledge of the West was being gained; but the great center of the country remained untouched. No settlement had been made beyond Ste. Genevieve, the first permanent white village in present Missouri.

In 1762, unknown to the venturesome French voyageurs, a secret treaty transferred Louisiana to the Spanish crown. Two years later St. Louis came into being, and the slow but steady westward march of the fur traders into the river country between the Mississippi and the Rocky Mountains gained impetus. Settlements began to appear on the west bank of the Mississippi around the mouth of the Missouri. By another secret switch, in 1800 Louisiana, now a pawn in the international chess game, was retroceded to France.

From then on matters moved more rapidly. On May 2, 1803, by the Treaty of Paris, Louisiana was sold to the burgeoning American Republic for approximately $15,000,000, or what figured out to be about four cents an acre. It was the greatest land transaction in history. But even before the Purchase, while the country was still a French possession, although administered by Spanish officials, President Jefferson had secured from Congress $2500 in secret funds for an expedition to ascend the Missouri, cross the Rocky Mountains, and descend to the Pacific.

In January, 1804, while the expedition, under Meriwether Lewis and William Clark, was in winter camp at Wood River, Illinois opposite the mouth of the Missouri, awaiting permission from Spanish officials at St. Louis to proceed, the news already in circulation of the sale of Louisiana to the United States was officially confirmed.

Soon after that, Major Amos Stoddard, U. S. A., came to St. Louis as joint agent of the United States and France in the formal transfer of Upper Louisiana, the lower region having been transferred at New Orleans in December, 1803.

At St. Louis on March 9, 1804, Don Carlos Dehault Dellassus, Spanish Lieutenant-Governor, formally transferred jurisdiction of Upper Louisiana to Stoddard, agent for France, who, the next day, surrendered it to himself as representative of the United States. That is the momentous event in American history whose centennial was marked by the Louisiana Purchase Exposition in St. Louis in 1904, and whose sesquicentennial we here help to celebrate.

What had the United States acquired? A claim to an immense and unmeasured expanse of land west of the Mississippi about which its people had very little actual knowledge; nominal sovereignty over its native population; a reputed abundance of wildlife; some rumors about mineral treasure; and a string of little settlements along the Mississippi, the eastern boundary. Could the United States hold this territory? The young Republic could and did. The land claim became a confirmed ownership and Louisiana was finally merged into the Union.

Louisiana Territory, as it was now called, turned out to be a roughly funnel-shaped empire of nearly 830,000 square miles, approximately bounded on the north by the Canadian frontier and the northeastern limit of the Missouri River valley; on the south by the Gulf of Mexico; on the east by the Mississippi River and the lake country about its head; and on the west by the Rocky Mountains, the Arkansas and Red Rivers. These, with the exception of the first, and a few other short arbitrary lines, were all natural boundaries. However, every limit of the Territory was subject to survey and adjustment. In terms of the developments that lay ahead the United States had acquired the states of Arkansas, Missouri, Iowa, South Dakota, Nebraska; all of Oklahoma but the Panhandle, all of Colorado east of the mountains except the far southeastern corner; all of Montana and Wyoming east of the Rockies; the whole of the Missouri River valley in North Dakota; all of Kansas but the far southwestern corner; all of Louisiana but the southwestern corner; a sliver of New Mexico and a splinter of the Texas Panhandle; and the gulf coasts of Mississippi and Alabama.

From the Mississippi delta swamps to the frozen peaks of the Rockies and the lakeland of the Chippewas, it was in climate, structure and resources an enormously diversified area. Its confines were the middle Rocky Mountain chain, with its spectacular landscape, hundreds of beaver streams and timbered foothill feed-grounds of the grizzly; the valley of the Arkansas, coming down through antelope meadows to touch the Cimarron Desert; the rust-colored Red River valley leading into the lush lower Mississippi lowlands; the wide and fertile west bank of the Mississippi; the forest glades of the northern lake country and the grotesque Dakota Bad Lands. In its heart were the Great Plains, accented by the Ozarks and the Black Hills, the whole area nourished by the Missouri and its tributaries.

Almost at once official exploring expeditions set forth into the wilderness. Their primary purpose was to provide first-hand information about the geography, peoples and resources of the new Territory. That of Lewis and Clark in 1804-1806 went to find a passage across the Rocky Mountains to the Pacific slope; those of Zebulon M. Pike in 1806-1807 to find the true source of the Missisisppi, and explore the Arkansas and Red River regions.

Although the results were not published until years later, much of the information brought back was generally known soon after they returned. Most interested, and first to act were the fur traders and trappers. From that time until about 1840, most of Louisiana Territory was their special province. They went west out of St. Louis and up the Missouri and the Platte and their affluents to explore, hunt, trade and build outposts of commerce. They found a land of grassy plains running out some distance short of the wooded foothills of the mountains, rivers of sometimes uncertain volume, an abundance of wild game, and Indians usually of uncertain temper. Away from the main watercourses it was virgin country that no white man had ever seen, and as they extended their wandering, they acquired the white man's first detailed knowledge of it.

To the pioneers, "crossing the plains" usually meant going from the Missouri River to one's destination, whether to the Rockies, or anywhere short of them. The Plains, for a hundred and fifty miles west of the junction of the Kaw and the Missouri, had a roll delightful to the eye; covered with an excellent growth of grass and wildflowers, they were bound to prove fertile. However, after that the pleasant undulations flattened out; the country became monotonous, and all that could be seen were less luxuriant grass and distance; and even before the traveler left this belt of the Plains, signs of the desert began to appear and multiply.

The trapper now came into a rather forbidding but, in a way, fascinating region: the broken, hilly belt that told him he was approaching the mountains, if indeed he could not make out in the distance their glistening crests. Rocky bluffs appeared along the streams, and remarkable carvings of nature stood boldly out, such as Court House Rock, Chimney Rock and Scott's Bluff in the valley of the North Platte, all famous landmarks on the Oregon trail, and mentioned by every traveler who went by that route and wrote of his trip. Farther north and in the same mood, the elements had sculptured the extensive, almost unbelievable, grotesqueries called the Bad Lands. Here, too, were dry alkali lakes completely without any form of life. "The early geographers," says Hiram M. Chittenden in *The American Fur Trade of the Far West*, "were not wrong in placing 'the Great American Desert' on their maps, much as they have been ridiculed for doing so. The error lay rather in its location and in their failure to note the many important exceptions."

As the trapper first came in sight of the Rockies he was apt to wonder whether those white masses athwart the sky were clouds or the snowy peaks of the mountains, but as he came closer and made out the gray outlines of their bulk, he knew that they were mountains and he was getting close to beaver country. Closer approach enabled him to see the timbered foothills, frequently grassy mountain slopes and parks, and dark conifer forests, reaching nearly to timberline. Considering all the ranges in what have been carelessly named the "Rocky Mountains," their highest pinnacles towered to nearly fifteen thousand feet. Pike's Peak and Long's Peak were the highest and most famous in Louisiana Territory. On the slopes of the Absaroka, Wind River, Bighorn, Medicine Bow, Front ranges, and the Black Hills, the trapper found the beaver streams for which he had traveled so many miles.

Within the ranges were parks and "holes," open grassy swales ringed by forests of pine, spruce and aspen, and refreshed by streams of cold clear water. These became well known to the trappers and most of them were usually named after their discoverers. The most famous were Jackson Hole, between the Absaroka and Wind River ranges; and South Park, between Pike's Peak and Long's Peak.

The progressively muddy Missouri River, originally the great highway to the West, has a rather gentle fall and ordinarily a slow meandering current. Its sources in the mountain streams of the far northwestern corner of Louisiana Territory are farther from the sea than those of any other American river, its whole course running more than four thousand miles. Its most important tributaries are the Yellowstone, the Platte and the Kaw, but the smaller sisters and feeders of these are countless. The operations of the American Fur Company, the biggest of all these enterprises, were largely conducted within the watershed of the Missouri, which the annals of the fur trade reveal as the most important natural adjunct to the trade. Years later, as cities, towns and villages dotted its course and farms rested upon its banks, it became more harmful than helpful when melting snows and spring rains swelled the Missouri into a rampant, tawny torrent that sought out every flat and depression and spread, miles wide, onto the cultivated lands and into the towns along its banks.

The Mississippi formed the eastern limit of Louisiana Territory, and for a distance of about twenty-five hundred miles marked that boundary. It is a much clearer stream than the Missouri, but at their confluence becomes and remains almost as turbid. It has, beside the Missouri (or does it in reality become the Missouri?) but two main affluents entering it from the west, both below the mouth of the Missouri: the Arkansas, which comes from the mountains and formed part of the southern boundary of the Territory, and the Red River, coming into the Mississippi not far from the Gulf of Mexico. The Mississippi, also, was an important adjunct to the fur trade; and parties of voyageurs from St. Louis ascended it to tap the rich resources of the northern fur country. But because of the keen competition from Canadian traders, the business done by Americans in that area never achieved the importance of the Rocky Mountain trade.

The vegetation of Louisiana Territory was extremely varied, from the conifers of the high mountains to the palmettos of the Gulf Coast. The most important tree of the Plains and perhaps of the West was the cottonwood, which grew along the low river banks. It was the typical Plains tree and sometimes the only one seen during long stretches of travel. The long lines of a cottonwood grove, with its probable indication of water, was a welcome sight to the trapper. The uses of the cottonwood were many. It gave gratifying shade, as well as fuel, and logs for shelter; its bark was nutritious food for horses, and its bole was used for the dugout canoes common on the Missouri and its tributaries. It also supplied palisades for the trading houses, almost always built as forts. In some localities on the Plains and in the foothills nearly impenetrable thickets of willows hugged the river flats, making trapping operations difficult. But the willow proved a necessity as an important food for the beaver and game, and a screen against human enemies. The mountain sides were covered with pine, spruce, fir, cedar and aspen, but these mountain forests, often dense, were obstacles to travel and of little use to the trapper. There were some well known belts of forest in Louisiana Territory: the Big Timbers on the north bank of the Arkansas, and the Cross Timbers sprawling across the watershed of the Canadian River.

The generally useless sagebrush was the most widespread of any plant of the Plains, and often, in the form of a dense miniature forest, was an impediment to travel. In a pinch it could be used for fuel, but its quick hot fire burned out swiftly. Greasewood, peculiarly, flourished in alkaline areas and farmers later learned that where the plant grew cultivation was profitless; but stockmen learned that it provided browsing for cattle and sheep where grass was scarce. Various species of cacti thrived on the semi-arid high plains even far to the north.

The grasses of the Plains were among the most important of their natural products. They provided food for all important herbiverous game, and for the domestic animals upon which the fur brigades largely traveled. Gramma, bunch and buffalo grasses were all first class feed for hoofed game and domestic animals, but of the three, bunch grass was the most nutritious both in summer and winter, and anything excellent in the West, of whatever nature, came to be called "bunch grass."

The profusion of wild fruits and edible roots in most parts of Louisiana Territory often helped allay hunger when other food was scarce. There were thickets of currants and many kinds of berries, and plum orchards. The camas root was a staple among the Indians, and sometimes a necessity for the trapper. Native maize fields were also to be found.

Kinikinik was introduced into the trapper's life by the Indian. This was usually ground from sumac leaves, red willow bark, or the leaves and bark of the bear berry, and mixed with trade tobacco. With a clay pipe stuffed and glowing with kinikinik, as the finished product was called, the trapper was "in town," and it often sufficed him as a sort of nourisher when there was no food at hand.

Herds of shaggy buffalo roamed the plains in such numbers that mile upon mile of prairie were covered with them. One hesitates to record the completely fantastic estimates of their numbers by competent experienced observers. Certainly there were millions. They provided the chief staple of food for both Indians and trappers, and afforded boats, tipi covers, robes, saddles, moccasin soles, and a great many other articles of domestic and military use, not forgetting the important buffalo chips or sun-dried dung, which gave fuel where no other fuel existed.

It was the demand for beaver fur in the world's markets that sent the trapper and trader into the inner and upper reaches of Louisiana Territory. Beaver fur was made into caps, and, in the form of felt, into the common beaver hat. When the beaver hat went out of fashion about 1833 and was supplanted by the silk hat, the beaver trade experienced a slump from which it never recovered. From this circumstance came a characteristic trapper *mot*: "Hell's full o' high silk hats."

The beaver, from every view point, is one of the most remarkable of animals: a dam-building engineer, a woodchopper, a house-builder, and a first-class navigator. Its house was built in water deepened by the construction of a dam, with the passage concealed under water, where much of the beaver's life was spent, and it was the trapper's job to lure it out with musk-bait arranged above the traps. With common beaver skins ranging around eight dollars apiece and a "plew" (prime skin) up to twelve dollars, there was great incentive in hunting it. To make its capture even more interesting was the rich feast provided by roast beaver tails, the mountains' greatest delicacy.

To add zest to his hunts, the trapper went after the great grizzly bear, the most ferocious of American wild beasts. Of all western game it was the most dangerous. The best thing to do with a grizzly was kill it with the first shot. Anything less than that could easily prove disastrous to the hunter, and there are many classic, well-authenticated tales about furious assaults upon trappers by wounded grizzlies that ended in death for the trapper, or a fearful mauling that crippled and disfigured him for life.

A typical plains animal was the odd, jerky little prairie dog, which congregated in towns that spread over many acres. It was a perennial source of interest to travelers, and accounts of it occupy many pages in the literature of the early West. The buffalo for food, the beaver for pelf, the grizzly for spice, the prairie dog for amusement.

And for food there were also the elk, next in importance to the buffalo for meat in bulk; the fleet, graceful antelope, provider of juicy steaks; the bighorn sheep, living high on the mountains, whose flesh was inferior to no wild meat; the peak-loving mountain goat; and the black bear which also made good steaks, and whose cubs made a delicious stew.

The wolf and mountain lion or panther, which the trapper called a "painter," were hunted for their skins; and the coyote, the night-prowling little "clean-up-man" of the Plains, was usually let alone to scavenge unmolested. Wild mustangs, often beautiful creatures descended from Spanish horses taken to Mexico by the *conquistadores*, ranged all over the West in herds of various sizes. Once roped, the mustang was tamed without much difficulty, but soon lost its wild beauty. Many were the western tales of milkwhite wild stallions so fleet no horsemen were ever able to capture them.

Widely scattered over Louisiana Territory were Indians of many tribes. The nature of the relationship between the Indians and the trappers and traders largely determined whether or not, in a chosen area, operations would be profitable. The Indian was also a trapper and hunter for profit, and the trade goods which he wanted were swapped for furs and peltry. Bartering with the Indians was an important part of the trade, and for this reason traders were always anxious to cultivate good relations with them.

Along the lower Missouri the Osages roamed the Ozark foothills. Farther north on the west bank lived the Pawnees, efficient horse thieves, and to the east of them across the river, were the Iowa villages. Still farther upriver roamed the various tribes of the great and powerful Sioux (or Dakota) nation, always more or less troublesome to the traders and trappers. North of the Sioux were the Mandan and Arikara towns, the former a friendly, agricultural people, the latter vacillating in their friendship, and the aggressors in several bloody fracases with the trappers.

The Assiniboines, a numerous people, were to be found on the approaches to the headwaters of the Missouri; and around the sources of the river ranged the tribes of the Blackfeet confederacy, a bold and warlike people. Both these nations, wandering in proximity to both American and British establishments, soon learned the advantage of playing off one group of traders against the other, and the Blackfeet particularly made many savage attacks upon the trappers operating in the headwaters country.

The tractable Flatheads, living up against the mountains in some of the best beaver country in the Territory, dwelt west of the Blackfeet, and south of them were the wily Crows and the Northern Cheyennes, both strong nations and not always friendly. The usually amiable Shoshonis lived in the country dominated by the Wind River Mountain chain, and had for their neighbors on the southeast the Arapahos and Southern Cheyennes. The Kiowas and Comanches made frequent incursions from the farther Southwest into the Arkansas River country and impinged upon the hunting grounds of the Southern Cheyennes.

In the southern end of Louisiana Territory lived less numerous peoples of another temperament, the Caddos, Quawpaws, Tunicas and Natchez; and in the northeastern corner of the Territory the Chippewas occupied a wide area extending from east of the Mississippi across the northern plains almost to the Missouri.

This was Louisiana Territory and these its denizens as first seen by the far-ranging trapper-discoverer as he penetrated into all its unknown parts, in his relentless search for beaver streams. He followed the mountain trails first trod by wild herds between feed-grounds and water. He and his close associate, the trader, were the true pioneers of the West. Here they met Indians they had never heard of, a few of whom took their coming kindly, some with doubt and apprehension and some with open hostility. It was usually the Indians, particularly those of the Blackfeet confederacy, encouraged by British traders, the Pawnees, Crows, Comanches, Arikaras, and the Sioux who provoked a dispute, regarding the white man as an intruder. However, almost all the tribes were at times troublesome, even the normally friendly Shoshonis.

The trapper's life was a rugged one, and only men of strength, intelligence, determination, courage, sharpened senses and good instincts, deep understanding of nature, and much better than average marksmanship survived. If the trapper lacked any of these and he had not the sense to go back home, his hair would soon decorate a hostile Indian lodge, while his body decayed in some lonely mountain canyon.

Up at chill dawn wading the icy mountain streams to set traps for the diabolically clever and elusive beaver, again wading back for the catch, if there was one, fighting the elements, eating whatever food he could find and sometimes close to starving, alert day and night to sudden Indian attack, spending long, lonely months in wild solitudes, the buckskin-clad Rocky Mountain trapper became a hardy, resolute, self-confident, far-ranging human being; he became and called himself a "mountain man."

Such were Old Bill Williams, Jim Bridger, the Sublettes, Tom Fitzpatrick, Joe Meek, Andrew Henry, Kit Carson and a score of others who stood tall above their fellows. They learned the West and taught it to the young greenhorns who showed up every season to learn the trade. Year after year the mountain men scoured the Rockies for new beaver water until, by 1840, before anybody ever heard of such official explorers as John C. Fremont, they had explored every nook of the Louisiana Territory (which by general consent and official acquiescence later became known as Missouri Territory, with a governor in St. Louis) and the country out to the Pacific.

In the early days of the fur trade, before the establishment of large, permanent trading posts where the trappers brought their furs and received their supplies, there came into being a typical outgrowth of the trade, the annual trappers' fair or "rendezvous." This institution, set up at a different site each year, accomplished the purpose of a trading post and provided the mountain man his recreation, which he liked rough and carnal. Here he got the reward for his hard work, and with his money or credits leaped forthwith into the ruggedest kind of play: drinking, fighting, gambling, horse racing, tests of skill and stamina with "no holts barred", shooting matches (many a battered old St. Louis-made Hawken Rifle "put 'er plumb center" and won a pot), squaw "doin's," and other forms of early Rocky Mountain entertainment. Everybody gathered at the rendezvous: seasoned mountain men, greenhorns, traders, whiskey runners, clerks, sportsmen, mixed-bloods, artists, writers, sometimes priests and preachers; and Indians, including young squaws, looking over the assembled mountain men for good providers.

At dusk the odors of roast buffalo hump, deer and antelope steaks and cub stew rose from the fires encircling the playground, floated through the alcoholic aroma and mingled with the sounds of boisterous feasting; for a trapper at rendezvous was a man "in town" and not one to stifle noisy evidence of his satisfactions. There the greenhorn learned "poor bull from fat cow;" and every mountain man was an after dinner speaker. Many a classic tall tale of the West was first conceived and told at rendezvous and ultimately found its way into the books, greatly enriching the literature of the fur trade. Everybody got so much out of the rendezvous that such gatherings were held until some years after the permanent trading posts were built: Fort Pierre, Fort Clark, and Fort Union on the upper Missouri; Fort Laramie, where plains and mountains meet; and Bent's Fort, on the upper Arkansas.

When the great demand for beaver skins ceased about 1840, the trapper was succeeded by the hide hunter who pursued the buffalo to practical extinction, shipping the hides to eastern markets to be made into winter coats, of which thousands were ordered by the Army for the use of soldiers on the Plains. The carcasses of the buffalo rotted on the prairie.

During the years of the fur trade's expansion into the farthest reaches of Louisiana Territory, a development was taking place at the same time in the lower country. The serious Indian troubles incident to the War of 1812 slowed the tempo of growth in the lower Missouri valley, and, for a time, halted operations of the fur trade. After the war, however, settlements continued to blossom in the lower Missouri and Mississippi valleys with populations that thought largely in terms of the West." Trade with Santa Fe was finally prospering, and, with the fur trade, brought wealth to St. Louis and Independence and the towns between. The lumbering freight wagons of the Santa Fe traders left the Missouri settlements and crossed the prairies of Kansas to the Arkansas River. Following this stream to the Cimarron Crossing they forded it there or at Bent's Fort on the "mountain branch" of the Santa Fe Trail, and continued their journey to the Southwest.

As the trails across the prairies and mountains became more deeply marked and better known, and maps and logs of western journeys commenced to appear, a thin migration of settlers and pioneering missionaries began in the late 'thirties. Their destination was known as the Oregon country, on the far side of the mountains. It was followed by a heavier Oregon migration in the middle 'forties; and later in that decade the Mormon migration crept across the Territory into the Promised Land. The surge of westward migration reached its peak in 1849 when gold hunters headed for California; but for several years after mid-century there was a heavy movement of settlers bound for the lands along the Pacific. Few of them settled in the old Territory. It was always: Westward! "On to Oregon!" "Ho, for California!"

Escorted by their armed, mounted menfolks and sometimes guided and guarded by old mountain men, now otherwise unemployed, long lines of ox-drawn, white-topped prairie schooners swung out from the settlements around the mouth of the Kaw, and wound across the Plains. With all their possessions, whole families and clans, including children and pets, were piled into the wagons. Most of the settlers went out by way of the Oregon Trail; up the country to the Platte River, up the Platte to the neighborhood of Fort Laramie, and from there onto the Sweetwater, across the mountains and into the Oregon country or down to California. At the time there were few permanent settlers' habitations in all that stretch. The military and commercial establishments were almost the only outposts of civilization along the route. Hardships awaited these journeying families along the trail: thirst, sickness and death, flooded streams, mud and quicksands, arid miles, hunger, worn-out animals, broken wagons, torrents and storms and choking dust, Indian attack, scarcity of grass and lack of firewood. Sometimes they were obliged to stop to care for the sick, or to bury the dead; sometimes they were forced to send out hunters far from the trail into Indian country for buffalo, antelope or whatever they could find to feed the camp; oxen got mired in quicksand and smothered to death; cattle often drowned in an attempt to cross a swollen stream, wagons capsized and whole cargoes were swept into the muddy swirls; sometimes played-out oxen had to be shot or abandoned, and frequently days were required to repair wagons and gear, mend tires or fashion new ones; at times the emigrants had to stop and huddle against the fearful prairie storms; not infrequently people and wagons and animals were corralled into a circle of defense against raiding Indians; and there were occasions when everybody in the train had to scatter out and hunt for buffalo chips, often the only fuel to be found.

Yet the trek had its happy side too: births, marriages, dances, music and singing, preaching, yarn swapping, practical joking, successful hunts and abundant fresh meat, children's games, long stretches of pleasant weather, ample pasturage, rising hopes. Many a youngster first saw the world inside a covered wagon; many a couple met, decided, and got married on the trail. A wedding celebration would follow with a "shivaree" and irrepressible jokesters. After the evening meal, a few of the men would haul out whatever "musical instruments" they could find (fiddles, banjos, flutes; or only a piece of paper and a comb, a whistle, a box or tub to pound) and swing into a lively old fiddle tune: "Oh Susannah," "Buffalo Gals," "Pop Goes the Weasel." Then when everybody got into the spirit of the thing, a "right smart parcel" of the young people would kick off their boots, step up, and go to "stompin' the prairie," while the musicians drew and strummed and blew and pounded, and everybody sang. On Sundays one of the men, a preacher if present, read out the gospel, preached, and led the prayers and hymns.

At night, while the horses and cattle grazed, the men and boys not on guard duty gathered round the fires and told stories and jokes; and if there was a mountain man around they were apt to hear some mighty tall tales most solemnly rendered—something to be remembered a lifetime. In the early evening the youngsters would shrill their little songs and romp through their games. There was great rejoicing, too, when after a long dry stretch, men riding ahead galloped back with news of fresh water; or when, after a time of starvation rations, the hunters rode into camp with big masses of freshly butchered buffalo beef, or sides of elk or antelope, or maybe, for spice, chunks of bear.

Slowly, steadily, interminably, day after weary day, the white caravans crawled across the old Territory bound for the Western promise —thousands of people and animals and wagons—a nation on the move. Through the late eighteen thirties, the 'forties and into the 'fifties it went on, year after year and through a vast unpopulated region, for it was not until the 'fifties that farms and settlements began to dot the Plains.

In 1858 gold was discovered where Cherry Creek runs into the South Platte. This was the future site of Denver. In that year a party of Cherokee Indians got into the high country north of Pike's Peak, and panned some "color." Word soon got around. People shouted "Pike's Peak or bust!" as they headed out and swarmed into the region and spread out into the mountains, where they tossed together a scattering of rakish mining camps. It was the beginning of the settlement of present Colorado, and the start of an expansive and colorful era.

About this time, too, the cattleman began to drive his herds into the old Territory to grow fat upon the nutritious grasses of the plains, founding an expansive industry that occupied great stretches of the West. It had its trail herds, cowpunchers, cow ponies and chuck wagons, its roundups, roping, and branding. Boisterous, often disreputable cowtowns sprang up at the railheads when the railroads came West, setting the pattern of life on the Plains for several decades.

To serve the miners and cattle men, public transportation and communication services were set up. Freight and express systems, stagecoach lines, and the Pony Express made a network across the old Territory and into the new settlements. During the War between the States these services facilitated the movement of army officers, gold, minted money, despatches and letters between Washington and the West.

The disturbances of war reverberated on the Plains. The powerful Sioux, under their war chief, Red Cloud, became restless and finally hostile. Travel was threatened or halted. The Army went in, built more forts, and had some desperate and bloody struggles before an uneasy truce was arranged. Meantime, in the early 'seventies gold was discovered in the Black Hills of South Dakota. Another stampede ensued—this time into country held sacred by the Sioux. The Army made gestures to stop the invasion, but the trouble came to a climax when General George A. Custer and his command were annihilated by the Sioux on the Little Bighorn River in 1876 in present Montana.

Part of the epic of Louisiana Territory is the story of the development of steam navigation on its great rivers. Following the early days of the bateau and the keelboat, heavy cumbersome vessels manually propelled by lusty, noisy crews, the Mississippi and Missouri entered upon the great age of the steamboat which reached its climax in the palatial craft familiar to every reader of Mark Twain. After some experimenting on the lower Mississippi, effective and regular steam service on the river may be said to have begun in 1817 with the voyage of the New Orleans steamer "General Pike." Practical steam navigation of the Missouri, inaugurated in 1819 by the fantastic government steamer "Western Engineer," added vigor to life along the river; and although steamers ran with fair regularity against the snags and sandbars and ultimately steamed as far upstream as Fort Benton in present Montana, the traffic never reached the extent of that on the Mississippi. River traffic with its later great and often luxurious sternwheel and sidewheel packets, developed into so important a phase of western life and commerce that most of the cities and towns up and down the river owe to it their real growth. For many years a colorful part of the western scene, steam navigation of the Mississippi has left us an extraordinary literature and a picturesque art.

The clamor for a trans-continental railroad had begun as early as the eighteen forties. It was more than twenty years later that the dream became a reality. The rails extended out from Omaha, at the mouth of the Platte, up that river and the South Platte, and into the mountains by way of Bridger's Pass to a point in Utah, where they met the end of another line which reached out to the east from Sacramento. The road for the iron horse was completed in 1869 against the opposition of the Indians. The event marked the end of the great freight wagons and the stagecoaches, and the beginning of a period of growth the West had not dreamed of.

As the last decades of the nineteenth century passed, what had been Louisiana Territory was rapidly filling with farms, mines, ranches, factories, cities and towns. Roads, railroads, and telegraph lines crisscrossed the country. On the cold, stark field of Wounded Knee the wild, free life of the West, as typified by the resisting Sioux, breathed its last.

Then it was 1900. The last frontier had vanished, and with it, the old West.

The Land: River, Plain and Mountain

 **W**HEN TITLE to the vast Louisiana Territory was delivered to the infant Republic of the United States in 1804, no part of its eight hundred and thirty thousand square miles of mountain, plain and river, except for New Orleans and its immediate environs, had ever been described in pictorial terms. By the close of the century that followed there was hardly an aspect of this dramatically varied immensity of land that had not inspired the artist's brush or pencil.

Meriwether Lewis and William Clark, when dispatched by President Jefferson in 1804 on an exploratory expedition westward across the newly acquired country, set forth into a wilderness. Except for the early Spanish and French explorers and the lonely French Canadian voyageurs, who for a hundred years had plied the rivers trapping the beaver, the great land lying between the Mississippi and the Rockies was virtually unknown to white men. Yet before a century had passed the last frontier had disappeared and the wilderness, representing about one-third of the United States, had become an integral part of the nation. Through these years an increasing demand for the image of the West stirred up the artist to venture beyond the Mississippi. The Territory offered boundless subject matter for landscape and gradually this *terra incognita* with its fabulous mountains, oceanic plains and endless waterways which had captured the imagination of the world was revealed in sketch book, on canvas and in countless prints from the lithographer's stone and the engraver's plate. This first section of the book presents a selection of these pictures which, until photography came into its own, were the sole means of forming the image of the West in the popular mind. Indeed, the better known amongst these paintings have taken so firm a place in our culture that our imaginations when the West is recalled cannot resist the power of their coloration.

Nineteen artists are represented in these pages. Their works range from the first modest topographic views in watercolor by Samuel Seymour to the grandiose oils of Thomas Moran. Amongst these men are some of the best known painters of nineteenth century America such as Catlin, Bingham, Whittredge and Bierstadt. Others are virtually unknown. Three were visiting Europeans.

In a surprising number of instances it was the Army or an official government expedition that provided the means of bringing the artist into contact with the West. In fact it was as an official member of Major Stephen H. Long's expedition to the foot of the Rockies that Seymour, the English-born topographic artist of Philadelphia, made the first landscapes beyond the Mississippi in 1819-1820. Similarly it was a United States geological survey that carried Thomas Moran into the fabulous region of the Yellowstone fifty years later and provided the inspiration for his most famous canvases that were based upon the atmospheric style of his idol, Turner, whose works he had studied in England. In the intervening years the Army brought Captain Seth Eastman to the upper Mississippi where he was stationed at Fort Snelling, and carried John Mix Stanley from Oklahoma Territory to the Pacific coast. The Government's northern railway survey later took Stanley to the West again from St. Paul. Albert Bierstadt, fresh home from his training in Düsseldorf, had his first experience with the West as a member of General F. W. Lander's surveying expedition in 1858, and in 1865-1866 Worthington Whittredge travelled West with General John Pope on his tour of inspection. In the latter year the remarkable Swiss artist, Frank Buchser, spent four months touring the valley of the Platte as a companion of General Sherman. Even the painter of the swamplands of the lower Mississippi, James R. Meeker, was introduced to this all-absorbing theme of his art by way of his tour with the armed services during the Civil War. And the rare and rather naive watercolors of Hermann Stieffel were a by-product of his years of service as an Army private in Kansas and Montana.

Two of the most important and productive artists of the West accompanied private expeditions across the Purchase Territory. These were Charles Bodmer, the Swiss who traveled with that veteran explorer and naturalist, the German princeling from the Rhineland, Maximilian, of Wied in 1833; and Alfred Jacob Miller who accompanied Sir William Drummond Stewart, the Scottish sportsman, in 1837. Fortunately for us they followed different routes. Maximilian and Bodmer voyaged up the Missouri beyond its confluence with the Yellowstone. Stewart and Miller took the westward trail following the Platte to its headwaters in the Rockies. One other explorer who was his own artist preceded them in 1822-1823. This was Prince Paul of Württemberg who traveled up the Missouri as guest of the American Fur Company and made the earliest known view of the river at a place which a few years later became the site of Fort Leavenworth, Kansas.

The landscape of the West was no less the inspiration of a number of artists who pursued the subject on their own. Amongst them are such remarkable figures as Catlin, Bingham and Blakelock as well as the lesser known Wimar, Wild and Alfred E. Mathews, the latter three of whom died at an early age. While Catlin's prevailing interest was the Indian in his natural habitat, he was so awed by the landscape of the West and so versatile as an artist that he could not resist recording in many canvases the mountains, plains, and riverscapes on his famous voyage up the Missouri in 1832. Bingham was the only artist who grew up amidst the scenes he painted. His occasional landscapes are based upon the Ozark mountain scenery of Missouri and would seem to represent an artistic relaxation from his more exacting compositions of river boatmen and political life. Likewise, Charles Wimar—especially in his beautiful drawings—was sometimes deflected from his absorption with the Indian and set down his impressions of the Plains and the banks of the Missouri. Ralph Blakelock spent the first of three years in the West in 1869. There he observed the Indians with a romantic idyllicism and made many sketches of the landscape of the Rockies, raw materials that were to serve him repeatedly in the poetic compositions of later years.

John Casper Wild, a Swiss who settled first in Philadelphia and later in St. Louis, became the first important landscape painter of the Mississippi and concentrated his sensitive vision on the young towns that were growing up along its shores. Alfred E. Mathews was born in England and like Wild, settled in the West. There he devoted himself to preserving the youthful image of the towns of Colorado as they were springing up amidst the imposing landscape of the Rockies.

[1]

Cliffs of Red Sandstone near the Rocky Mountains
By Samuel Seymour. 1820

"This extensive range, rising abruptly from the plain, skirts the base of the mountains like an immense rampart . . . It is made up of rocks composed of the broken down . . . fragments of pre-existing aggregates, embosoming reliquae of the animals of a former world, known to us only by the monuments which these remains exhibit . . . We observed here several singular scorpion-like, spider-formed animals, inhabiting under stones and dried bison's dung."

Edwin James, *Account of an Expedition from Pittsburg to the Rocky Mountains in 1819, 1820* (1823)

[2]

View of the Arkansas near the Rocky Mountains
By Samuel Seymour. 1820

"This is, next to the Missouri, the largest and most interesting tributary of the Mississippi, and from its mouth by its meanders to the mountains, is commonly computed about two thousand miles. Its course has been traced in these mountains at least five hundred miles, and it is believed that the sources of the Arkansas have not yet been explored by our people. One singularity distinguishes this river from any other of the United States. Where it winds along among the mountains, all agree that it is a broad and deep river, and carries a great volume of water. But no sooner does it emerge from the shelter of woods and mountains, into a boundless and arid plain,—composed to a great depth of quicksands,—than it begins to disappear; and in a hundred miles from the very elevated mountain, near which it enters upon the plain, it is fordable during the summer. Still lower down it is a stream, according to the well-known phrase of this country, 'sunk in the sand;' that is, it trickles amidst the banks of sand and pebbles, so as in many places to exhibit a dry channel of burning sand from bank to bank. Here, on these vast sandy plains, which will for ages be the Syrtes of America, the home of elks and buffaloes, are the wide fields of those rich native grapes, that all travelers in these regions have spoken of in terms of such admiration."

Frederick Marryat, *A Diary in America* (1839)

[3]

View of the Missouri at Wasa-bae Wakanda-ge
LITHOGRAPH AFTER A SKETCH BY PRINCE PAUL OF WURTTEMBERG. 1823

"The winding river, with its islands, willow bordery, and groves of cotton-wood trees, the whole scene in fact, had something magnificent, though melancholy. I was reminded how much I must yet traverse before I can reach the end of the voyage. On this side (S.W.) I found the soil of the upland of an excellent quality, and, notwithstanding the ravages of the fire, the marks of which are every where to be seen, the woods, principally hickory, ash, oak, and walnut, formed a forest tolerably close."

H. M. Brackenridge, *Journal of a Voyage up the River Missouri in 1811* (1814)

This is the earliest known view of the Missouri; four years later it became the site of Fort Leavenworth (Kansas). Formerly the site of a Kansas Indian village it was known by the fur traders as *le Village de Douce* (Village Twelve) as it was twelve hours travel from the mouth of the Kansas.

[4]

Prairie Fire
By George Catlin. 1832

"But there is yet another character of burning prairies—the war, or hell of fires: where the grass is seven or eight feet high, as is often the case for many miles together, on the Missouri bottoms; and the flames are driven forward by the hurricanes, which often sweep over the vast prairies of this denuded country. There are many of these meadows on the Missouri, the Platte, and the Arkansas . . . The fire in these, before such a wind, travels at an immense and frightful rate, and often destroys, on their fleetest horses, parties of Indians . . . not that it travels as fast as a horse at full speed, but that the high grass is filled with wild pea-vines and other impediments, which render it necessary for the rider to guide his horse in the zig-zag paths of the deers and buffaloes . . . until he is overtaken by the dense column of smoke that is swept before the fire—alarming the horse, which stops and stands terrified and immutable, till the burning grass which is wafted in the wind, falls about him, kindling up in a moment a thousand new fires, which are instantly wrapped in the swelling flood of smoke that is moving on like a black thunder-cloud, rolling on the earth, with its lightning's glare, and its thunder rumbling as it goes."

George Catlin, *North American Indians* (1841)

[5]

Cliffs on the Upper Missouri
By Charles Bodmer. 1833

"There is, much of the way on one side or the other, a bold and abrupt precipice of three or four hundred feet in elevation, presenting itself in an exceedingly rough and picturesque form, to the shore of the river; sloping down from the summit level of the prairies above, which sweep off from the brink of the precipice, almost level, to an unknown distance.

"It is along the rugged and wild fronts of these cliffs, whose sides are generally formed of hard clay, that the mountain-sheep dwell, and are often discovered in great numbers."

George Catlin, *North American Indians* (1841)

[6]

Curious Formations on the Upper Missouri
By Charles Bodmer. 1833

"Amongst these groups may be seen tens and hundreds of thousands of different forms and figures, of the sublime and the picturesque; in many places for miles together, as the boat glides along, there is one continued appearance, before and behind us, of some ancient and boundless city in ruins—ramparts, terraces, domes, towers, citadels and castles may be seen,—cupolas, and magnificent porticoes, and here and there a solitary column and crumbling pedestal, and even spires of clay which stand alone—and glistening in the distance, as the sun's rays are refracted back by the thousand crystals of gypsum which are embedded in the clay of which they are formed. Over and through these groups of domes and battlements (as one is compelled to imagine them), the sun sends his long and gilding rays, at morn or in the evening; giving life and light, by aid of shadows cast to the different glowing colours of these clay-built ruins; shedding a glory over the solitude of this wild and pictured country, which no one can realize unless he travels here and looks upon it."

George Catlin, *North American Indians* (1841)

[7]

Snags on the Missouri
Aquatint after a drawing by Charles Bodmer. 1839

" . . . but piloting becomes another matter when you apply it to vast streams like the Mississippi and the Missouri, whose alluvial banks cave and change constantly, whose snags are always hunting up new quarters, whose sand-bars are never at rest, whose channels are forever dodging and shirking, and whose obstructions must be confronted in all nights and all weathers without the aid of a single lighthouse or a single buoy; for there is neither light nor buoy to be found anywhere in all this three or four thousand miles of villainous river."

Mark Twain, *Life on the Mississippi* (1874)

[8]

Confluence of the Yellowstone and Missouri Rivers
AQUATINT AFTER A DRAWING BY CHARLES BODMER. 1839

"Following the numerous windings of the Missouri, from one chain of hills to another, we reached, at seven o'clock in the evening, the mouth of the Yellow Stone, a fine river, hardly inferior in breadth to the Missouri at this part. It issues below the high grey chain of hills, and its mouth is bordered with a fine wood of tall poplars, with willow thickets. The two rivers unite in an obtuse angle; and there is a sudden turn of the Missouri to the north-west; it is not wooded at the junction, but flows between prairies thirty or more miles in extent. Herds of buffaloes are often seen here; at this time they had left these parts: we saw, however, many antelopes. At the next turn of the river, towards the right hand, we had a fine prospect. Gentle eminences, with various rounded or flat tops, covered with bright verdure, formed the back-ground; before them, tall poplar groves, and willow thickets on the bank of the river, whose dark blue waters, splendidly illuminated by the setting sun, flowed, with many windings, through the prairie."

Maximilian, Prince of Wied, *Travels in the Interior of North America* (1843)

[9]

Prairie
By Alfred Jacob Miller. 1837

"The view of these prairies is often compared to that of the sea, and the comparison is correct. There is the same boundless sweep to the eye, with rolling waves of green from horizon to horizon—the same undulating play of sunshine and shade on its face—the same solitude—the same solemn and silent grandeur. And the resemblance in its features of life are not dissimilar. A distant wagon is a sail, and wrecks strew its strands as they do the ocean's shores. Bones of animals that have perished by the wayside line the route, and, of themselves, tell you of the scores of thousands that have passed on this great highway to the Pacific."

J. F. Meline, *Two Thousand Miles on Horseback* (1867)

"Before us were the treeless plains of green, as they had been since the flood —beautiful, unbroken by bush or rock; unsoiled by plow or spade; sweetly scented with the first blossomings of Spring. They had been since time commenced, the theatre of the Indian's prowess—of his hopes, joys, and sorrows . . . The grass was now (May) four inches in height and bent in rows in most sprightly beauty under the gusts of wind which at intervals swept over."

Thomas Farnham, *Travels in the Great Western Prairies, the Anahuac and Rocky Mountains and in Oregon Territory* (1843)

[10]

Scott's Bluff near the Platte
By Alfred Jacob Miller. 1837

"By the aid of a little ideality, these objects can be easily molded into temples, towers, steeples, forts, castles and ampitheaters. I was not prepared to find that Nature had here, along the banks of the lonely Platte, a river unknown to song, wrought upon such a scale of grandeur, where beauty and sublimity are combined in a manner truly wonderful.

"The base of the bluffs along here, consists of a clay or marl, nearly white, while the summit often consists of strata of horizontal rocks. We encamp for the night about three miles east of Scott's Bluff, so called on account of a man by the name of Scott, who died under peculiar circumstances and whose mortal remains lie entombed at its base. This man was taken sick, and his party, in order to save their own lives, were obliged to leave him to perish alone, although at his own request. Scott's Bluff appears, from the spot where I now sit, like an immense castle, two hundred feet high and a mile square, with battlements, towers and redoubts flanking it around on all sides."

Franklin Langworthy, *Scenery of the Plains, Mountains and Mines* (1855)

[11]

The Devil's Gate
By Alfred Jacob Miller. 1837

"We encamp for the night near the Devil's Gate, so called—not a very agreeable neighborhood, if we were judged by the name. At this place the Sweet Water rushes down a tremendous chasm, forming a most terrific pass through a mountain of rock, which seems to have been rent asunder by some convulsion in nature."

Franklin Langworthy, *Scenery of the Plains, Mountains and Mines* (1855)

[12]

Lake Scene. Wind River Mountains
By ALFRED JACOB MILLER. 1837

"From the right a promontory or bluff projects out boldly into the midst of the Lake throwing a broad reflection into the water,—beyond this the mountains begin to rise until they reach their ultimatum in cold barren peaks of solid rock covered with snow. Although it was the month of August, we had frequent snow and hail storms, and towards evening thick overcoats were almost indispensable to comfort. In the morning one or two of the hunters would be dispatched for mountain sheep, or any other game of a size to warrant a shot, for powder and ball are precious articles here and not to be wasted; others would scramble out on the rocks to catch the finny-tribe, not solely for amusement, —no indeed!—keen appetites and insatiable maws were in expectancy, and always ready to do justice to either fish or flesh, with a blazing fire burning briskly, 'in case (as Wilkins Micawber, has it) anything should turn up.' After the meal we could then sit patiently and listen to some Trapper relating reminiscences of his adventures, —his huntings, and fightings with the Indians, and his loves with Indian beauties forming the principal ground work of his narrative."

Alfred Jacob Miller, *Notes* (1837) quoted in *The West of Alfred Jacob Miller*, edited by Marvin C. Ross, 1951

[13]

High Water in the Bayou Country
BY AN UNKNOWN ARTIST. About 1840

"At certain seasons the Mississippi overflows its banks, at all those places where no Levees have been made. During the latter end of April, and the beginning of May, when we passed along, we found the river flowing over the western side, for the distance of several hundred miles."

Basil Hall, *Forty Etchings, from Sketches made with the Camera Lucida, in North America* (1829)

[14]

View of Davenport, Iowa and the Mississippi
By J. C. WILD. 1844

"It is surely no misnomer that this giant stream has been styled the 'eternal river,' the 'terrible Mississippi;' for we may find none other imbodying so many elements of the fearful and the sublime. In the wild rice-lakes of the far frozen north, amid a solitude broken only by the shrill clang of the myriad water-fowls, is its home. Gushing out from its fountains clear as the air-bell, it sparkles over the white pebbly sand-beds, and, breaking over the beautiful falls of the 'Laughing Water,' it takes up its majestic march to the distant deep. Rolling onward through the shades of magnificent forests, and hoary, castellated cliffs, and beautiful meadows, its volume is swollen as it advances, until it receives to its bosom a tributary, a rival, a conqueror, which has roamed three thousand miles for the meeting, and its original features are lost for ever. Its beauty is merged in sublimity! Pouring along in its deep bed the heaped-up waters of streams which drain the broadest valley on the globe; sweeping onward in a boiling mass, furious, turbid, always dangerous; tearing away, from time to time, its deep banks, with their giant colonnades of living verdure, and then, with the stern despotism of a conqueror, flinging them aside again; governed by no principle but its own lawless will, the dark majesty of its features summons up an emotion of the sublime which defies contrast or parallel."

Edmund Flagg, *The Far West* (1838)

[45]

Dubuque, Iowa
LITHOGRAPH AFTER A PAINTING BY J. C. WILD. About 1845

"We noticed that above *Dubuque* the water of the Mississippi was olive-green—rich and beautiful and semi-transparent, with the sun on it. Of course the water was nowhere as clear or of as fine a complexion as it is in some other seasons of the year; for now it was at flood stage, and therefore dimmed and blurred by the mud manufactured from caving banks.

"The majestic bluffs that overlook the river, along through this region, charm one with the grace and variety of their forms, and the soft beauty of their adornment. The steep, verdant slope, whose base is at the water's edge, is topped by a lofty rampart of broken, turreted rocks, which are exquisitely rich and mellow in color—mainly dark browns and dull greens, but splashed with other tints. And then you have the shining river, winding here and there and yonder, its sweep interrupted at intervals by clusters of wooded islands threaded by silver channels; and you have glimpses of distant villages, asleep upon capes; and of stealthy rafts slipping along in the shade of the forest walls; and of white steamers vanishing around remote points. And it is all as tranquil and reposeful as dreamland, and has nothing this-worldly about it—nothing to hang a fret or a worry upon."

Mark Twain, *Life on the Mississippi* (1874)

[16]

The Laughing Waters
By Seth Eastman. About 1845

"One of the curiosities of our vicinity . . . is the Minne-Ha-Ha or the Laughing Water, called also Brown's Falls. It is situated west of the Mississippi, and distant about three miles from Ft. Snelling. Ten miles above the falls the stream flows from Lake Calhoun and it passes through a level but fertile prairie, its margin decked with a wholesome growth of willow, poplar, and hazel, while at a short distance there are little forests of blackjack and other trees of like character. Here the sheet of water is from twenty to twenty-five feet wide and its fall forty-one feet. The rock over which it pours shelters an oval cave about seventy-five feet wide and thirty feet from the falling water to the back. Though the magnitude of this cascade is not such as to excite our wonder, its picturesque beauty and pleasing melody attract the admiration of every visitor."

Isaac I. Stevens, *Reports of Surveys for a Railroad from the Mississippi to the Pacific* (1853-55)

Falls of St. Anthony
BY SETH EASTMAN. About 1845

"With the common propensity of travellers to exaggerate, the Falls of St. Anthony, until very recently, have been much overrated. Instead of the extravagant estimates of the French writers, or the fall of fifty feet assigned to them by more modern authorities; the real fall of the Mississippi here is between sixteen and seventeen feet of perpendicular descent. Though it has not the slightest claim to compare with that of Niagara in grandeur, it furnishes an impressive and beautiful spectacle in the loneliness of the desert. The adjoining scenery is of the most striking and romantic character; and as the traveller listens to the solemn roar of the falls, as it sinks into feeble echoes in the forests, a thrilling story is told him of the love and despair of a young Dacota Indian woman, who, goaded by jealousy towards her husband, who had taken another wife, placed her young children in a canoe, and chanting the remembrances of love and broken vows, precipitated herself and her infants down the falls."

Timothy Flint, *The History and Geography of the Mississippi Valley* (1831)

[18]

The Storm
By George Caleb Bingham. About 1850

The "thunderstorm . . . had an old-fashioned energy which had long been unfamiliar to me. This third storm was accompanied by a raging wind . . . The wind bent the young trees down, exposing the pale underside of the leaves; and gust after gust followed in quick succession, thrashing the branches violently up and down, and to this side and that . . . No color that was visible anywhere was quite natural—all tints were charged with a leaden tinge from the solid cloud-bank overhead . . . The thunder-peals were constant and deafening; explosion followed explosion with but inconsequential intervals between, and the reports grew steadily sharper and higher-keyed, and more trying to the ear; the lightning was as diligent as the thunder, and produced effects which enchanted the nerve in the body in unintermittent procession. . . .

"People boast a good deal about Alpine thunderstorms; but the storms which I have had the luck to see in the Alps were not the equals of some which I have seen in the Mississippi Valley. I may not have seen the Alps do their best, of course, and if they can beat the Mississippi, I don't wish to."

Mark Twain, *Life on the Mississippi* (1874)

[19]

Western Landscape
By JOHN MIX STANLEY. Probably 1853

"The Sweetwater is a tributary of the Platte, taking its rise in the neighboring mountains where it is fed by melting snow. Its clear, cool water, which was highly appreciated by our party after having so long used the turbid waters of the Platte, and the broad valley which afforded splendid grazing for our animals, with large quantities of driftwood which furnished fuel for cooking, and the grand view of distant mountain, besides other interesting objects near by, combined to make it a camping place at which we would have liked to remain for a week."

Reuben Cole Shaw, *Across the Plains in Forty-nine* (1896)

[20]

Mountain Lake
By Albert Bierstadt. After 1858

"The most favorable time to view these Lakes (to an artist especially) was early in the morning or towards sunset;—at these times one side or the other would be thrown into deep purple masses, throwing great broad shadows, with sharp light glittering on the extreme top,—while the opposite mountains received its full complement of warm, mellow and subdued light;—thus forming a *chiaro obscuro* and contrast most essential to the picturesque in color:—an attempt has been made to reach this in the sketch. This was the only lake we saw that had an island;—the scene in reality was charming, but would have required the pencil of a Stanfield, Turner, or Church in giving it due effect and rendering it complete justice. Patiently it awaits the coming man."

Alfred Jacob Miller, *Notes* (1837) quoted from *The West of Alfred Jacob Miller*, edited by Marvin C. Ross, 1951

Western Sunset
By ALBERT BIERSTADT. After 1858

"The belt of country, partially wooded, extends generally from two to four hundred miles west of the Mississippi and its waters. There commences that ocean of prairies, that constitutes so striking and impressive a feature in the vast country beyond the Mississippi and Missouri. This vast country is for the most part a plain, more or less covered with grass, in great extents; in other extents almost a moving sand. It is pastured and trodden by countless number of buffaloes, elk, and other wild animals that graze upon it. In some places, as on the Missouri, spurs of the mountains are encountered long before we reach the main ridge."

Timothy Flint, *The History and Geography of the Mississippi Valley* (1831)

"As you proceed toward the west from the Missouri, the size of the trees diminishes, as well as the number of kinds. As you penetrate the borders of the Indian country, leaving civilization behind you, the sight of forests is no longer enjoyed, the only trees to be seen being scattered along the banks of the streams, these becoming smaller and more rare, finally disappearing altogether and giving place to a few scattering willows and osiers. The greater portion of the Plains may be said to be without timber of any kind."

George A. Custer, *My Life on the Plains* (1874)

[22]

Jenny Lake, Wyoming
By ALBERT BIERSTADT. About 1860

"Who can paint the mountains, the seas or the skies? And if Bierstadt could reproduce on canvas this miracle of the heavens, the art critics would say: 'It is utterly impossible—no living man ever looked upon such skies!' He who sees truly will no more place limits upon the wonders of the universe than upon the divine love which pervades and suffuses it. In nature, as in human life, nothing is impossible."

Albert D. Richardson, *Beyond the Mississippi* (1867)

[23]

Wind River Country, Wyoming
By ALBERT BIERSTADT. 1861

"It was the 20th of July, that Captain Bonneville first came in sight of the grand region of his hopes and anticipations, the Rocky mountains. He had been making a bend to the south, to avoid some obstacles along the river, and had attained a high, rocky ridge, when a magnificent prospect burst upon his sight. To the west, rose the Wind river mountains, with their bleached and snowy summits towering into what appeared to be faint clouds, but which the experienced eyes of the veteran hunters of the party recognised for the rugged mountains of the Yellowstone; at the feet of which, extended the wild Crow country: a perilous, though profitable region for the trapper . . .

"We can imagine the enthusiasm of the worthy captain, when he beheld the vast and mountainous scene of his adventurous enterprise thus suddenly unveiled before him. We can imagine with what feelings of awe and admiration he must have contemplated the Wind river sierra, or bed of mountains; that great fountain head, from whose springs, and lakes, and melted snows, some of those mighty rivers take their rise, which wander over hundreds of miles of varied country and clime; and find their way to the opposite waves of the Atlantic and the Pacific."

Washington Irving, *The Rocky Mountains* (1837)

[24]

Cottonwoods on the Missouri
By CHARLES WIMAR. 1858

". . . there is a redeeming beauty in the green and carpeted shores, which hem in this huge and terrible deformity of waters. There is much of the way though, where the mighty forests of stately cotton wood stand, and frown in horrid dark and coolness over the filthy abyss below; into which they are ready to plunge headlong, when the mud and soil in which they were germed and reared has been washed out from underneath them, and is with the rolling current mixed, and on its way to the ocean."

George Catlin, *North American Indians* (1841)

"The banks are almost always nearly perpendicular, and are seldom more than two or three feet above the surface of the water at its present high stage, so that the work of devastation is constantly going on. The river is at once deep, swift, and generally narrow—hardly so wide in the average as the Hudson below Albany, though carrying the water of thirty Hudsons. . . . Its muddiness is beyond all description; its color and consistency are those of thick milk porridge; you could not discern an egg in a glass of it. A fly floating in a teacup of this dubious fluid an eighth of an inch below the surface would be quite invisible."

Horace Greeley, *An Overland Journey, from New York to San Francisco* (1860)

[25]

White Castles on the Missouri
BY CHARLES WIMAR. 1858

"As soon as we have passed Judith River this white sand-stone begins to stand out in some places, till we have passed Bighorn River, and entered the narrower valley of the Stone Walls, where the strata extend, without interruption, far through the country, and lie partly halfway up the mountain, and partly form the summits. They are the continuation of the white sand-stone which occurs in such singular forms at the Blackhills. At all the places which are bare of grass, they are visible, and there we see horizontal or perpendicular angles and ledges resembling walls, some of which contain caverns. This sandstone formation is the most striking when it forms the tops of more isolated mountains, separated by gentle valleys and ravines. Here, on both sides of the river, the most strange forms are seen, and you may fancy that you see colonnades, small round pillars with large globes or a flat slab at the top, little towers, pulpits, organs with their pipes, old ruins, fortresses, castles, churches, with pointed towers, etc., etc., almost every mountain bearing on its summit some similar structure."

Maximilian, Prince of Wied, *Travels in the Interior of North America* (1843)

[26]

Buttes on the Missouri
BY CHARLES WIMAR. 1858

"Long tracts of the sand-stone strata perfectly resembled a large blown-up fortress, because the stratification every where gave these walls a certain regularity, while, at the same time, they bore marks of having been destroyed by violence. In several places where the sand-stone summit appeared plainly to represent an ancient knight's castle, another remarkable rock was seen to traverse the mountain in narrow perpendicular strata, like regularly built walls."

Maximilian, Prince of Wied, *Travels in the Interior of North America* (1843)

Western Landscape
BY THOMAS MORAN. 1864

"These magnificent changes in mountain scenery occasioned by light and shade during one of these terrific tempests, with all the incidental accompaniments of thunder, lightning, rain, snow and hail, afford the most awe-inspiring exhibition in nature. As I write, another grand storm, which does not extend to our camp, has broken out on Emigrant peak, which at one moment is completely obscured in darkness; at the next, perhaps, brilliant with light; all its gorges, recesses, seams and canyons illuminated; these fade away into dim twilight, broken by a terrific flash, and, echoing to successive peals,

> ' . . . the rattling crags among
> Leaps the live thunder' in innumerable reverberations."

Nathaniel P. Langford, *Diary of the Washburn Expedition to the Yellowstone and Firehole Rivers* (1871)

[28]

On the Platte
BY FRANK BUCHSER. 1866

"We had a Swiss artist, M. Buchser, sent over by his government to make a grand painting illustrative of our late war, embracing our most famous statesmen and generals, for the Capitol at Berne. Having a month or two of leisure, he was spending it wisely in making a run to the Plains and the Rocky Mountains. Now he was hurrying on to join Gen. Sherman at Julesburg, whence he was to accompany him and his brother, the Ohio Senator, on a tour of inspection to Fort Laramie, Buford, Denver, and then east again via the Arkansas. He was a close observer, had travelled much on both continents, and was very chatty and companionable, speaking English like a native. He sketched constantly en route, making 'studies' of the Platte valley from the top of the stage-coach . . ."

James F. Rusling, *Across America* (1874)

[29]

The Lonesome Rider
By Frank Buchser. 1866

". . . from Laramie I have followed the regular California and Oregon Overland Trail, already many times described, and by this time familiar to hundreds of thousands. Suffice it that, for over two hundred miles from Laramie, it traverses a region substantially described in my notes of my journey from the buffalo-range to Denver, and from Denver to Laramie; a region, for the most part, rainless in summer and autumn, yet on whose soil of more or less sandy clay, lacking support from ridges of underlying rock, has been more seamed, and gouged, and gullied, and washed away, by the action of bluffs and buttes, and deep ravines, and intervales, and shallow alkaline lakelets, now mainly dried up, and streams running milky, even when low, when the clay gullied from their banks, and sent off to render the Missouri a river of mud, and to fertilize the bottoms of the lower Mississippi."

Horace Greeley, *An Overland Journey, from New York to San Francisco* (1860)

In the Rockies
BY WORTHINGTON WHITTREDGE. About 1865

"In the little valley of fifteen or twenty acres, nestling between mountain peaks, we found everything needed for our comfort. Even the deer, which furnished the meat for our dinner, was captured on the spot by the hunters who were in advance of our train. The valley was pronounced the most picturesque mountain park yet seen, and many of our party would have liked to camp there for a day. There was no timber within view except small evergreens and thickets of service-berry bushes . . . About two hours were spent in that mountain retreat, which proved to be a fine field for students in geology, while in these little valleys, with rare plants in brilliant bloom, the botanist loves to linger."

Reuben Cole Shaw, *Across the Plains in Forty-nine* (1896)

[31]

Crossing the Ford—Platte River, Colorado
BY WORTHINGTON WHITTREDGE. 1870

"The overland travel from the states to Oregon and California will find its great highway along its banks. The Platte, therefore, when considered in relation to our intercourse with the habitable countries on the western ocean assumes an unequalled importance among the streams of the great prairie wilderness. But for it, it would be impossible for man or beast to travel those arid plains, destitute alike, of wood, water and grass, save what of each is found along its course. On the headwaters of the north fork, too, is the only way or opening in the Rocky Mountains at all practicable for a carriage road through them."

Thomas J. Farnham, *Travels in the Great Western Prairies, the Anahuac and Rocky Mountains and in the Oregon Territory* (1843)

Rocky Mountains
By Ralph Blakelock. About 1870

"Bierstadt, it is said, made some beautiful drawings of these rocks, but refused to paint them, giving as his reason that few people would believe they were real rocks of this continent, and would say he had taken some foreign ruins and tried to palm them off on the public as specimens of Colorado rock-scenery. Since seeing them, I am not surprised at his conclusion."

A. K. McClure, *Three Thousand Miles through the Rocky Mountains* (1869)

"I have read somewhere (I think in Washington Irving's 'Astoria' or 'Bonneville's Adventures') that the Indians regard this ridge of mountains as the crest of the world, and that among the Blackfeet there is a fable that he who attains its summit catches a view of the 'Land of Souls' and beholds the 'Happy Hunting Grounds' spread out below him, brightening with the abodes of the free and generous spirits."

Nathaniel P. Langford, *Diary of the Washburn Expedition to the Yellowstone and Firehole Rivers* (1871)

In the Swamp Opposite Bayou Sara
By Joseph R. Meeker. 1872

"There cannot be well imagined another feature to the gloom of these vast and dismal forests, to finish this kind of landscape, more in keeping with the rest, than the long moss, or Spanish beard, and this funereal drapery attaches itself to the cypress in preference to any other tree. There is not, that I know, an object in nature, which produces such a number of sepulchral images as the view of the cypress forests, all shagged, dark, and enveloped in the hanging festoons of moss. . . .

"This curious appendage to the trees is first visible in the cypress swamps at about thirty-three degrees, and is seen thence to the Gulf. It is the constant accompaniment of the trees in deep bottoms and swampy lands, and seems to be an indication of the degree of humidity in the atmosphere. I have observed that in dry and hilly pine woods, far from streams and stagnant waters, it almost wholly disappears; but in the pine woods it reappears as you approach bottoms, streams, and swamps. I have remarked too, that where it so completely envelopes the cypress, as to show nothing but the festoons of the dark grey moss, other trees are wholly free from it. It seems less inclined to attach itself to the cotton wood trees, than to any others."

Frederick Marryat, *A Diary in America* (1839)

The Wichita Mountains from the Medicine Bluffs
BY HERMANN STIEFFEL. About 1879

"Unlike most mountains, the Wichita cannot properly be termed a range or chain, but more correctly a collection or group, as many of the highest and most beautiful are detached, and stand on a level plain, solitary and alone. They are mainly composed of granite, the huge blocks of which exhibit numerous shades of beautiful colors, crimson, purple, yellow, and green predominating. They are conical in shape, and seem to have but little resemblance to the soil upon which they are founded. They rise abruptly from a level surface—so level and unobstructed that it would be an easy matter to drive a carriage to any point of the circumference at the base; and yet so steep and broken are the sides that it is only here and there that it is possible to ascend them. From the foot of almost every mountain pours a stream of limpid water, of almost icy coldness."

George A. Custer, *My Life on the Plains* (1874)

[35]

The Yellowstone River near Fort Keough, Montana
By HERMANN STIEFFEL. 1879

"We left Fort Keough on the morning of the 30th of August. Our route took us up the Yellowstone some twelve miles through a series of as picturesque bad lands as are to be found anywhere in the West. Their bald, rugged, ever-changing forms and outlines rendered an otherwise uneventful ride interesting in the extreme. . . .

"Just before reaching the creek we struck the Keough stage trail, a tolerably fair road leading from Bismark to Fort Keough. There is a line of stages, so called, buckboards in fact, running between these two points, which carry the mail, express matter, and any passengers who have courage enough to risk their scalps in making the trip. They run every day so that Fort Keough, Miles City, and other towns situated from three to five hundred miles west of Bismark, get daily mails when the weather or Indians don't interfere."

G. O. Shields, *Rustlings in the Rockies* (1883)

[36]

Hot Springs near the Yellowstone
By Thomas Moran. 1871-73

"Six miles above the upper fall we entered upon a region remarkable for the number and variety of its hot springs and craters. The principal spring, and the one that first meets the eye as you approach from the north, is a hot sulphur spring, of oval shape, the water of which is constantly boiling and is thrown up to the height of from three to seven feet. . . . This spring is situated at the base of a low mountain and the gentle slope below and around the spring for the distance of two hundred or three hundred feet is covered to the depth of from three to ten inches with the sulphurous deposit from the overflow of the spring. The moistened bed of a dried-up rivulet, leading from the edge of the spring down inside through this deposit, showed us that the spring had but recently been overflowing. Farther along the base of this mountain is a sulphurous cavern . . . out of which the steam is thrown in jets with a sound resembling the puffing of a steam-boat when laboring over a sand-bar, and with as much uniformity and intonation as if emitted by a high-pressure engine. From hundreds of fissures in the adjoining mountain from base to summit, issue hot sulphur vapors, the apertures through which they escape being encased in thick incrustations of sulphur, which in many instances is perfectly pure. There are nearby a number of small sulphur springs, not especially remarkable in appearance."

Nathaniel P. Langford, *Diary of the Washburn Expedition to the Yellowstone and Firehole Rivers* (1871)

[37]

Giant Blue Spring, Yellowstone Region
BY THOMAS MORAN. 1873

"But the most remarkable of all the springs at this point are six or seven of a character differing from any of the rest. The water in them is of a dark blue or ultra-marine hue, but it is wonderfully clear and transparent. Two of these springs are quite large; the remaining five are smaller, their diameters ranging from eight to fifteen feet. . . . The largest two of these springs are irregular in their general outline of nearly an oval shape, the larger of the two being about twenty-five feet wide by forty long, and the smaller about twenty by thirty feet."

Nathaniel P. Langford, *Diary of the Washburn Expedition to the Yellowstone and Firehole Rivers* (1871)

[38]

Cliffs of the Green River, Wyoming Territory
BY THOMAS MORAN. 1882

"Our camp here is a most lovely one in every respect, and as several days have elapsed since we came, and I am convalescent, I can roam about the country a little and enjoy it. The pasture is rich and very abundant, and it does our hearts good to witness the satisfaction and comfort of our poor jaded horses. Our tents are pitched in a pretty little valley or indentation in the plain, surrounded on all sides by low bluffs of yellow clay. Near us flows the clear deep water of the Siskadee, and beyond, on every side, is a wide and level prairie, interrupted only by some gigantic peaks of mountains and conical *butes* in the distance. The river, here, contains a great number of large trout, some grayling, and a small narrow-mouthed white fish, resembling a herring. They are all frequently taken with the hook, and, the trout particularly, afford excellent sport to the lovers of angling. Old Izaac Walton would be in his glory here, and the precautionary measures which he so strongly recommends in approaching a trout stream, he would not need to practise, as the fish is not shy, and bites quickly and eagerly at a grasshopper or minnow."

John K. Townsend, *Narrative of a Journey Across the Rocky Mountains* (1839)

The Indian

O F ALL THE phases of the life of the West that were radically altered or destroyed by the Purchase of Louisiana, none held greater fascination for the artist than the Indian. The European especially was intrigued by the savage who figured largely in both the written and the pictorial record of the visiting foreigner. And to this day no primitive aspect of the region continues so steadfastly to command our imagination. The Indian, in fact, is still virtually synonymous with the West. In Jefferson's administration thousands of Indians of many tribes roamed the huge mid-continent region purchased from France, or lived in villages like the Mandans and Minitarees in North Dakota. By 1900, despoiled of their primeval holdings and their wild freedom, they existed only in reservations under sufferance of the Government. Meanwhile it was the artist who, at prodigious expense of endurance, patience and tact, and with countless miles of travel, created a precious record of the Indians of the Plains in their natural state before that life disappeared with the closing of the last frontier. A large part of American Indian ethnology is based upon this record. The most important contributors were the great painters of the Indian: Catlin, Bodmer, Eastman and Stanley who were chiefly active in the 'thirties, 'forties and 'fifties. But there were numerous others both famous and obscure who helped to complement this unexampled pageant. Many of the best of these painters we represent in the pages that follow.

As in the case of the landscape of the West, it was also the obscure Samuel Seymour, emerging from his conventional studio and engraver's shop in Philadelphia, who first painted the Plains Indians in 1819-1820 as a member of Major Long's expedition to the Rockies. He was followed by the scarcely less obscure Peter Rindisbacher, the youthful Swiss immigrant, who observed the redmen of Minnesota, North Dakota and Wisconsin and was the first artist to represent the mounted buffalo hunt of the Indian. Meantime, in Washington, the

War Department had established the "Indian Gallery" which for some fifteen years was to amass a great number of portraits of chiefs of the Plains tribes that were painted on their visits to the Capital. The majority are the work of Charles Bird King. One of the first and perhaps the finest of them is the group portrait that appears here, painted in 1821.

The decade of the 'thirties saw the prodigious activity of Catlin in the West and the long visit of Charles Bodmer. The tireless Catlin, inspired to paint all the Indian tribes of North America before they should vanish "to the shades of their fathers," voyaged up the Mississippi, then up the Missouri, and then went south to Arkansas and New Orleans. For eight years he traveled, painting upwards of five hundred canvases of Indians, landscapes and wild life. Less productive, but far more painstaking and subtle in his craft, was Charles Bodmer who, in the employ of Maximilian of Wied, paused in New Orleans in 1833 long enough to paint the Choctaw Indians, a familiar sight on the streets of the city, and then the following year accompanied the naturalist Prince up the Missouri beyond the confluence of the Yellowstone. His watercolor drawings of the Plains tribes made on this trip are unsurpassed and the beautiful published aquatints that stemmed from them and illustrated Maximilian's book, are a milestone in American ethnology. One can only regret that the Prince did not also on this voyage indulge his artistic bent, for he himself was a documentary artist of great ability. He apparently met Rindisbacher in St. Louis and acquired from him three of his watercolors of Indians. Four years later in Baltimore Alfred Jacob Miller, having met his patron, Captain William Drummond Stewart, in New Orleans spent six months in the Platte Valley and the Rockies creating, in the sophisticated romantic style he had acquired in Paris, a record of the Plains Indians that is almost as impressive as that of his two distinguished predecessors.

The trail blazers of the 'thirties were followed by Captain Seth Eastman, the West Pointer and teacher of drawing at the Military Academy who was stationed at Fort Snelling in the 'forties and who applied his skill primarily in painting the Indians of Minnesota. His important contribution consists not only of his carefully composed oil paintings, but of many watercolors which were reproduced as illustrations to his wife's books on the Indians and Henry M. Schoolcraft's famous six-volume work, *The Indian Tribes of the United States*.

John Mix Stanley was almost as widely traveled as Catlin. He traversed the Southwest and the Northwest and visited California and Hawaii as well as the upper Mississippi where at Fort Snelling he had decided as early as 1840 to make the depiction of the Indian his life work. Happily he was chosen as official artist and photographer of Governor Isaac Stevens' northern railway surveying expedition in 1853 which yielded the fine lithographic illustrations in the published report.

In the same decade the German-born Wimar, who had grown up in St. Louis and studied at Düsseldorf, filled his sketchbooks with drawings on his Missouri voyages and from them created some of the most authentic interpretations of Indian life that exist.

Only once in his known work did Bingham relax his interest in landscape, Missouri politics and the life of the boatman to paint a purely Indian subject. This picture, *The Concealed Enemy*, representing an Osage brave in ambush, was painted about 1850 and is here published for the first time.

The Indian was of little more than incidental interest as part of the Western scene to the artists of the generation that followed, such as Bierstadt, Frank Buchser the visiting Swiss painter, Hermann Stieffel the Army private, and Paul Frenzeny the French illustrator who is primarily known for his pictorial reporting for *Harper's Weekly*. It was not until the end of the century in the work of Frederic Remington that the Indian as he still existed on the Plains assumed a major role in the production of an artist of the West.

[39]   [40]

Mandan Man and Woman
By C. B. J. F. de Saint-Memin. 1804

"The Mandans are certainly a very interesting and pleasing people in their personal appearance and manners; differing in many respects, both in looks and customs, from all other tribes which I have seen. They are not a warlike people, for they seldom, if ever, carry war into their enemies' country; but when invaded show their valor and courage to be equal to that of any people on earth. . . . There is certainly great justice in the remark, and so forcibly have I been struck with the peculiar ease and elegance of these people, together with the diversity of complexions, the various colors of their hair and eyes, the singularity of their language, and their peculiar and unaccountable customs, that I am fully convinced that they have sprung from some other origin than that of the North American tribes, or that they are an amalgam of natives with some civilized race. . . .

"A stranger in the Mandan village is first struck with the different shades of complexion and various colors of hair which he sees in a crowd about him, and is at once almost disposed to exclaim that 'these are not Indians.' There are a great many of these people whose complexions appear as light as half-breeds; and amongst the women particularly there are many whose skins are almost white, with the most pleasing symmetry and proportion of features; with hazel, with gray, and with blue eyes; with mildness and sweetness of expression, and excessive modesty of demeanor, which render them exceedingly pleasing and beautiful."

George Catlin, *Notes* quoted in *The George Catlin Indian Gallery*, by Thomas Donaldson, 1885

[74]

Pawnee Council
BY SAMUEL SEYMOUR. 1820

"On the following day the Pawnees were summoned to council, and in a short time they appeared . . . The Indians arranged themselves on the benches prepared for them . . .

"Major O'Fallon arose and addressed them in a very austere tone and manner, stating the offences they had committed against the white people, and admonishing them to a reformation in their conduct . . .

"In concluding his address, . . . Major O'Fallon requested them, if any subject rested heavily on their minds, to come forward and express themselves without fear. Long-hair (Tarrarecawaho) placed himself in the middle of the area. He stood for a short time immovable, then slowly advanced nearer to the agent (O'Fallon), and with a very loud, powerful voice, fierce countenance, and vehement gesticulation, . . . addressed him . . ."

Edwin James, *Account of an Expedition from Pittsburg to the Rocky Mountains in 1819, 1820* (1823)

"The present number of this tribe [Pawnees] is ten or twelve thousand; about one half the number they had in 1832, when that most appalling disease, the small-pox, was accidentally introduced among them by the Fur Traders, and whiskey sellers; when ten thousand (or more) of them perished in the course of a few months."

George Catlin, *North American Indians* (1841)

Dog Dance of the Kansas Indians
BY SAMUEL SEYMOUR. 1820

"In the evening they now retired to rest in the lodge set apart for their accommodation, when they were alarmed by a party of savages rushing in, armed with
bows, arrows and lances, shouting and yelling in a most frightful manner . . .
The Indians collected around the fire in the centre of the lodge, yelling incessantly; . . . After singing for some time, one who appeared to be their leader,
struck the post over the fire with his lance, and they all began to dance, keeping
very exact time with the music. Each warrior had, besides his arms, and rattles
made of strings of deers' hoofs, some part of the intestines of an animal inflated,
and enclosing a few small stones, which produced a sound like pebbles in a
gourd shell. After dancing around the fire for some time, without appearing
to notice the strangers, they departed, raising the same wolfish howl with which
they had entered; but their music and their yelling continued to be heard about
the village during the night."

Edwin James, *Account of an Expedition from Pittsburg to the Rocky Mountains
in 1819, 1820* (1823)

[43]

Young Omahaw, War Eagle, Little Missouri and Pawnees
By CHARLES BIRD KING. 1821

"The colour of these Indians is a fine brown, sometimes reddish, more or less dark, which might, sometimes, come under the denomination of copper colour. In some it is more of a greyish-brown, in others yellowish; after a thorough ablution the skin of some of them appears almost white, and even some colour in their cheeks. They do not disfigure their bodies, only they make some apertures in the outer rim of the ear, in which they hang strings of beads, brass or iron rings of different sizes, or shells, the last of which they obtain from other Indian tribes. If they are questioned respecting these shells, they answer that they were brought from the sea. These Indians are vain, and in this respect childish, like all savage nations. They are very fond of ornament. . . ."

Maximilian, Prince of Wied, *Travels in the Interior of North America* (1843)

[44]

Shaumonekusse, Chief of the Otoes
BY CHARLES BIRD KING. About 1830

"Just so a white man travels amongst a wild and untaught tribe of Indians, and sees occasionally one of them parading about their village, with a head-dress of eagle's quills and ermine, and elevated above it a pair of beautifully polished buffalo horns."

George Catlin, *North American Indians* (1841)

"The Mandans and Manitaries, and all the Indians of the Upper Missouri, often wear the handsome necklace made of the claws of the grizzly bear. These claws are very large in the spring, frequently three inches long, and the points are tinged of a white colour, which is much esteemed; only the claws of the fore feet are used for necklaces."

Maximilian, Prince of Wied, *Travels in the Interior of North America* (1843)

[45]

"No Heart"—Ioway
By Charles Bird King. 1837

"In short, he is the greatest coxcomb on the face of the earth, not to be surpassed even in London for inordinate vanity, stupendous egotism, and love of self. His features may not be strictly classical, according to our standard of beauty. His cheek-bones might be considered somewhat too prominent, and his paint certainly is inadmissible with us: but, to do him justice, I must allow that he is not a bad-looking fellow in his way."

The Earl of Dunraven, *The Great Divide* (1876)

[46]

Inside of an Indian Tent
By Peter Rindisbacher. 1824

" . . . entered several lodges, the people of which received us with kindness, placed mats and skins for us to sit on, and after smoking the pipe, offered us something to eat; this consisted of fresh buffaloe meat served in a wooden dish. They had a variety of earthen vessels, in which they prepared their food, or kept water."

H. M. Brackenridge, *Journal of a Voyage up the River Missouri in 1811* (1814)

[47]

Indians Returning from War
BY PETER RINDISBACHER. 1825

"The scalping is an operation not calculated of itself to take life, as it only
removes the skin, without injuring the bone of the head; and necessarily, to be
a genuine scalp, must contain and show the crown or centre of the head; that
part of the skin which lies directly over what the phrenologists call 'self-esteem,'
where the hair divides and radiates from the centre; of which they all profess
to be strict judges, and able to decide whether an effort has been made to produce
two or more scalps from one head. Besides taking the scalp, the victor generally
if he has time to do it without endangering his own scalp, cuts off and brings
home the rest of the hair, which his wife will divide into a great many small
locks, and with them fringe off the seams of his shirt and his leggings . . .
which also are worn as trophies and ornaments to the dress, and then are
familiarly called 'scalp-locks'."

George Catlin, *North American Indians* (1841)

Buffalo Hunting in Summer
BY PETER RINDISBACHER. About 1825

". . . it has been estimated that for each buffalo robe transported from the Indian country at least five animals are destroyed . . . . From the Missouri region, the number of robes received varies from 40,000 to 100,000 per annum, so that from a quarter to a half a million of buffalo are destroyed in the period of each twelve months. So enormous a drain must soon result in the extermination of the whole race; and it may be asserted with certainty that in twenty years from this time, the buffalo, if existing at all, will be only found in the wildest recesses of the Rocky Mountains. The savage bands of the West, whose progenitors have from time immemorial depended mainly upon the buffalo, must, with them, disappear from the earth, unless they resort to other means of subsistence, under the fostering care of the general government."

Randolph B. Marcy, *Thirty Years of Army Life on the Border* (1866)

[49]

Indians Hunting Buffalo
BY PETER RINDISBACHER. About 1825

"They are excellent horsemen—they will shoot an arrow at full speed, and again pick it up from the ground without stopping; sometimes they will lean entirely upon one leg, throwing their bodies to that side, so as to present nothing but the leg and thigh on the other. In pursuit of the buffaloe, they will gallop down steep hills, broken almost into precipices. Some of their horses are very fine, run swiftly, and are soon worn out, from the difficulty of procuring food for them in winter, the smaller branches of the cottonwood tree being almost the only fodder which they give them. Their hunting is regulated by the warriors chosen for the occasion, who urge on such as are tardy, and repress often with blows, those who would rush on too soon. When a herd of buffalo is discovered, they approach in proper order, within half a mile, they then separate and dispose themselves, so as in some measure, to surround them, when at the word, they rush forward at full speed, and continue the chase as long as their horses can stand it: a hunter usually shoots two arrows into a buffaloe, and then goes in pursuit of another; if he kills more than three in the hunt, he is considered as having acquitted himself well. The tongue is the prize of the person who has slain the animal; and he that has the greater number, is considered the best hunter of the day."

H. M. Brackenridge, *Journal of a Voyage up the River Missouri in 1811* (1814)

[50]

War Dance of the Sauks and Foxes
By Peter Rindisbacher. About 1829

"Dancing is among the most prominent of the aboriginal ceremonies. There is no tribe in which it is not practised. . . . In the war dance the actors are distinguished by a more free use of red and black paint. . . . The paint, in all the dances, is put on according to the fancy of each individual. . . .

"The music consists of a monotonous thumping with sticks upon a rude drum, accompanied by the voices of the dancers, and mingled with the rattling of gourds containing pebbles, and the jingling of small bells and pieces of tin, worn as ornaments. . . .

"The War Dances are pantomimic representations of the incidents of border warfare, and, although by no means attractive in themselves, become highly picturesque when contemplated in connection with their significant meaning. The persons engaged are warriors, the leaders of the tribe, and the great men of the day; and the allusions are to the heroic deeds or subtle stratagems of themselves, or their ancestors, or to some danger that threatens, or some act of violence about to be perpetrated."

Thomas L. McKenney and James Hall, *The Indian Tribes of North America* (1827-43), edited by F. W. Hodge, 1933

This painting and the succeeding one by Rindisbacher were apparently acquired from the artist by Maxmilian, Prince of Wied, when he stopped in St. Louis in 1833.

Indian Dance
BY PETER RINDISBACHER. About 1829

"Dancing, I have before said, is one of the principal and most valued amuse-ments of the Indians, and much more frequently practised by them than by any civilised society; inasmuch as it enters into their forms of worship, and is often their mode of appealing to the Great Spirit—of paying their usual de-votions to their *medicine*—and of honouring and entertaining strangers of distinction in their country.

"Instead of the 'giddy maze' of the quadrille or the country dance, enlivened by the cheering smiles and graces of silkened beauty, the Indian performs his rounds with jumps, and starts, and yells much to the satisfaction of his own exclusive self, and infinite amusement of the gentler sex, who are alway lookers on, but seldom allowed so great a pleasure, or so signal an honour, as that of joining with their lords in this or any other entertainment."

George Catlin, *North American Indians* (1841)

"Black Hawk"

BY GEORGE CATLIN. 1832

". . . I have been to Fort Jefferson, about nine miles from this, to see the famous Black Hawk, and his fellow chiefs, taken in the recent Indian war. This redoubtable Black Hawk, who makes such a figure in our newspapers, is an old man, upward of seventy, emaciated and enfeebled by the sufferings he has experienced, and by a touch of cholera. He has a small, well-formed head, with an acquiline nose, a good expression of eye; and a physician present who is given to craniology, perceived the organ of benevolence strongly developed, though I believe the old chieftain stands accused of many cruelties. His brother-in-law, the prophet, is a strong, stout man, and much younger. He is considered the most culpable agent in fomenting the late disturbance; though I find it extremely difficult, even when so near the seat of action, to get at the right story of these feuds between the white and red men, and my sympathies go strongly with the latter."

The Western Journals of Washington Irving (1832), edited by John Francis McDermott, 1944

[53]

View on the Upper Missouri—Riccaree Village
By George Catlin. 1832

" . . . a view of the Riccaree village, which is beautifully situated on the west bank of the river, 200 miles below the Mandans; and built very much in the same manner; being constituted of 150 earth-covered lodges, which are in part surrounded by an imperfect and open barrier of piquets set firmly in the ground, and of ten or twelve feet in height.

"This village is built upon an open prairie, and the gracefully undulating hills that rise in the distance behind it are everywhere covered with a verdant green turf, without a tree or a bush anywhere to be seen. This view was taken from the deck of the steamer when I was on my way up the river; and probably it was well that I took it then, for so hostile and deadly are the feelings of these people towards the *pale faces*, at this time, that it may be deemed most prudent for me to pass them on my way down the river, without stopping to make them a visit. They certainly are harbouring the most resentful feelings at this time towards the Traders, and others passing on the river; and no doubt, that there is great danger of the lives of any white men, who unluckily fall into their hands. They have recently sworn death and destruction to every white man, who comes in their way; and there is no doubt, that they are ready to execute their threats."

George Catlin, *North American Indians* (1841)

Buffalo Chase
BY GEORGE CATLIN. 1832

"These horses are so trained that the Indian has little use for the rein, which hangs on the neck, whilst the horse approaches the animal on the right side, giving his rider the chance to throw his arrow to the left, which he does at the instant when the horse is passing, bringing him opposite to the heart, which receives the deadly weapon 'to the feather.' When pursuing a large herd the Indian generally rides close in the rear until he selects the animal he wishes to kill, which he separates from the throng as soon as he can by dashing his horse between it and the herd and forcing it off by itself, where he can approach it without the danger of being trampled to death, to which he is often liable by too closely escorting the multitude."

George Catlin, *North American Indians* (1841)

Buffalo Hunt, Under the Wolf Mask
BY GEORGE CATLIN. 1832

"The poor buffaloes have their enemy *man*, besetting and besieging them at all times of the year, and in all the modes that man in his superior wisdom has been able to devise for their destruction. They struggle in vain to evade his deadly shafts, when he dashes amongst them over the plains on his wild horse— they plunge into the snow-drifts where they yield themselves an easy prey to their destroyers, and they also stand unwittingly and behold him unsuspected under the skin of a white wolf, insinuating himself and his fatal weapons into close company when they are peaceably grazing on the level prairies, and shot down before they are aware of their danger.

". . . While the herd of buffaloes are together they seem to have little dread of the wolf, and allow them to come in close company with them. The Indian takes advantage of this fact, and often places himself under the skin of the animal and crawls for half a mile or more on his hands and knees until he approaches within a few rods of the unsuspecting group, and easily shoots down the fattest of the throng."

George Catlin, *North American Indians* (1841)

[56]

Scalp Dance
By George Catlin. 1832

"The Scalp-dance is given as a celebration of a victory; and amongst this tribe, as I learned whilst residing with them, danced in the night, by the light of their torches, and just before retiring to bed. When a war party returns from a war excursion, bringing home with them the scalps of their enemies, they generally 'dance them' for fifteen nights in succession, vaunting forth the most extravagant boasts of their wonderful prowess in war, whilst they brandish their war weapons in their hands. A number of young women are selected to aid (though they do not actually join in the dance), by stepping into the centre of the ring, and holding up the scalps that have been recently taken, whilst the warriors dance (or rather *jump*), around in a circle, brandishing their weapons, and barking and yelping in the most frightful manner, all jumping on both feet at a time, with a simultaneous stamp, and blow, and thrust of their weapons; with which it would seem as if they were actually cutting and carving each other to pieces. During these frantic leaps and yelps, and thrusts, every man distorts his face to the utmost of his muscles, darting about his glaring eye-balls and snapping his teeth, as if he were in the heat (and actually breathing through his inflated nostrils the very hissing death) of battle! No description that can be written, could ever convey more than a feeble outline of the frightful effects of these scenes enacted in the dead and darkness of night, under the glaring light of their blazing flambeaux; nor could all the years allotted to mortal man, in the least obliterate or deface the vivid impress that one scene of this kind would leave upon his memory."

George Catlin, *North American Indians* (1841)

[57]

Snow-shoe Dance of the Ojibbeway
By George Catlin. About 1835

"Many were the dances given to me on different places, of which I may make further use and further mention on future occasions; but of which I shall name but one at present the *snow-shoe dance*, which is exceedingly picturesque, being danced with the snow-shoes under the feet, at the falling of the first snow in the beginning of winter; when they sing a song of thanksgiving to the Great Spirit for sending them a return of snow, when they can run on their snow shoes in their valued hunts, and easily take the game for their food."

George Catlin, *North American Indians* (1841)

[58]

"The Blue Medicine"
BY GEORGE CATLIN. 1835

"By the side of him *Toh-to-wah-kon-da-pee* (the blue medicine), a noted medicine-man, of the Ting-tah-to-a band; with his medicine or mystery drum, made of deer-skins; and his mystery rattles made of antelope's hoofs, in his hands. This notorious old man was professionally a doctor in his tribe, but not very distinguished, until my friend Dr. Jarvis, who is surgeon for the post, very liberally dealt out from the public medicine-chest, occasional 'odds and ends' to him, and with a *professional concern* for the poor old fellow's success, instructed him in the modes of their application; since which, the effects of his prescriptions have been so decided amongst his tribe, whom he holds in ignorance of his aid in his mysterious operations; that he has risen quite rapidly into notice, within the few last years, in the vicinity of the Fort; where he finds it most easy to carry out his new mode of practice, for reasons above mentioned."

George Catlin, *North American Indians* (1841)

[59]

"He who Drinks the Juice of the Stone"
BY GEORGE CATLIN. 1836

"The mode in which these sticks are constructed and used will be seen in the portrait of *Tullock-chish-ko* (he who drinks the juice of the stone), the most distinguished ball-player of the Choctaw nation, represented in his ball-play dress, with his ball-sticks in his hands. In every ball-play of these people it is a rule of the play, that no man shall wear moccasins on his feet, or any other dress than his breech-cloth around his waist, with a beautiful bead belt, and a 'tail,' made of white horse-hair or quills, and a *mane* on the neck, of horse-hair, dyed of various colors."

George Catlin, *North American Indians* (1841)

[60]

"Sam Perryman"
By George Catlin. 1836

"The Creeks until quite recently occupied . . . Mississippi and Alabama; but by . . . arrangement . . . with the Government, have exchanged their possessions there for a country, adjoining to the Cherokees, on the south side of the Arkansas . . . on which, like the Cherokees, they are laying out fine farms, and building good houses in which they live; in many instances, surrounded by immense fields of corn and wheat.

". . . I have given the portraits of two distinguished men . . both chiefs . . 'Ben Perryman' and . . . 'Sam Perryman.' These two men are brothers, and are fair specimens of the tribe, who are mostly clad in calicoes, and other cloths of civilized manufacture; tasselled and fringed off by themselves in the most fantastic way; and sometimes with much true and picturesque taste. They use a vast many beads, and other trinkets, to hang upon their necks, and ornament their moccasins and beautiful belts."

George Catlin, *North American Indians* (1841)

Indian Pipe-Smoker
BY CHARLES BODMER. 1833

"They wore their hair loosely hanging down their backs; none had shaved their heads; and, on the whole, they looked very dirty and miserable . . . Their noses, in general [are] rather longer . . . The men carried in their hands their tobacco pipes, made of red or black stone (a hardened clay), adorned with rings of lead or tin, which they generally obtain from the Sioux, at a high price."

Maximilian, Prince of Wied, *Travels in the Interior of North America* (1843)

Choctaw Indian in Blanket with   [62]
Powder Horn and Pouch

Choctaw Indian in White Man's   [63]
Shirt and Blue Waistcoat

Choctaw Indian in White Man's Ruffled Shirt [64]

New Orleans Indians
BY CHARLES BODMER. 1833

"These Indians who crawl about New Orleans are of the Choctaw tribe, and are a sort of outcasts, the fag end of the tribe, the selvage, the intermediate existence between annihilation and savage vigor. These sort of people appear to have existed here and made the city their camp before the surrender of the country to the United States, altho', as I am informed, they are much deteriorated in appearance and morals since the American whiskey arrived along with the American Government.

"The Indians strolling about New Orleans are generally extremely dirty and disgusting in their appearance. In the morning men are seen half clothed . . . Later in the day they appear, some of them painted, with feathers in their hair, wrapt up in blankets of different degrees of dirtiness.

"Towards noon men and women have sold their game or skins, have bought whiskey, and are *hocksy*, that is, half, or quite drunk. They stroll about quietly, and interrupt no one, and in fact their dirty appearance, long black greasy hair, and savage faces are the worst parts of them."

Benjamin H. B. Latrobe, *Impressions Respecting New Orleans* (1818-1820), edited by Samuel Wilson, Jr., 1951

[65]

Winter Village of the Minitarees
AQUATINT AFTER A DRAWING BY CHARLES BODMER. 1839

"The extensive white plain is enlivened by neither man nor beast, unless, indeed, some herds of buffaloes are in the neighborhood, or a few hungry wolves are prowling about in search of food. At that season there is generally more life on the frozen river, as the Indians are continually going backwards and forwards from their winter to their summer villages, and to the fort. Men, women, children, and dogs, drawing little sledges, are seen on it all day long; and the people of the fort amuse themselves with skating, and the children with sledges, especially on Sundays."

Maximilian, Prince of Wied, *Travels in the Interior of North America* (1843)

[66]

Minitaree Warrior in Costume of the Dog Dance
AQUATINT AFTER A DRAWING BY CHARLES BODMER. 1839

"Among the Mandans, and all the nations of the Upper Missouri, . . . there are certain bands or unions or companies, which are distinguished from the others, and kept together by certain external badges and laws. . . .

"The fourth band, that of the dogs, wear in their dance a large cap of coloured cloth, to which a great number of raven's, magpie's, and owl's feathers is fastened, adorned with dyed horsehair and strips of ermine; they have a large war pipe of the wing bone of a swan. . . . The head is generally adorned with a thick tuft of feathers hanging down behind, and often all the three kinds of feathers are mixed together. The three men before-mentioned, who wear the strips of red cloth (the dogs, properly so called), are obliged, if any one throws a piece of meat into the ashes, or on the ground, saying, 'There, dog, eat,' to fall upon it, and devour it raw, like dogs or beasts of prey. The schischikué of this band is a stick, a foot or a foot and a half long, to which a number of animals' hoofs are fastened."

Maximilian, Prince of Wied, *Travels in the Interior of North America* (1843)

The Interior of the Hut of a Mandan Chief
AQUATINT AFTER A DRAWING BY CHARLES BODMER. 1839

"The Mandans are undoubtedly secure in their villages, from the attacks of any Indian nation, and have nothing to fear, except when they meet their enemy on the prairie. Their village has a most novel appearance to the eye of a stranger; their lodges are closely grouped together, leaving but just room enough for walking and riding between them; and appear from without, to be built entirely of dirt; but one is surprised when he enters them, to see the neatness, comfort, and spacious dimensions of these earth-covered dwellings. They all have a circular form, and are from forty to sixty feet in diameter. . . . On the top of, and over the poles forming the roof, is placed a complete mat of willow-boughs, . . . and . . . a hard or tough clay, which is impervious to water, and which with long use becomes . . . a lounging place for the whole family in pleasant weather— for sage—for wooing lovers—for dogs and all; an airing place—a look-out—a place for gossip and mirth.

"The floors of these dwellings are of earth, but so hardened by use, and swept so clean, and tracked by bare and moccasined feet, that they have almost a polish, and would scarcely soil the whitest linen."

George Catlin, *North American Indians* (1841)

[68]

Tombs of Assiniboin Indians
Aquatint after a drawing by Charles Bodmer. 1839

"They believe in a creator, or lord of life (Unkan-Tange), and also in an evil spirit (Unkan-Schidja), who torments people with various disorders, against which their sorcerers or physicians (medicine men) use the drum and the rattle to expel the evil spirit. . . . They believe that the dead go to a country in the south, where the good and brave find women and buffaloes, while the wicked or cowardly are confined to an island, where they are destitute of all the pleasures of life. Those who, during their lives, have conducted themselves bravely, are not to be deposited in trees when they die, but their corpses are to be laid on the ground, it being taken for granted that, in case of need, they will help themselves. Of course they are then generally devoured by the wolves, to secure them from which, however, they are covered with wood and stones. Other corpses are usually placed on trees, as among the Sioux, and sometimes on scaffolds. They are tied up in buffalo hides, and three or four are sometimes laid in one tree."

Maximilian, Prince of Wied, *Travels in the Interior of North America* (1843)

[69]

Indian Pursuit
BY ALFRED JACOB MILLER. About 1840

"An Indian, therefore, mounted on a fleet and well-trained horse, with his bow in his hand, and his quiver slung on his back, containing an hundred arrows, of which he can throw fifteen or twenty in a minute, is a formidable and dangerous enemy. Many of them also ride with a lance of twelve or fourteen feet in length, with a blade of polished steel; and all of them (as a protection for their vital parts), with a shield or arrow-fender made of the skin of the buffalo's neck, which has been smoked and hardened with glue extracted from the hoofs. These shields are arrow-proof, and will glance off a rifle-shot with perfect effect by being turned obliquely, which they do with great skill."

George Catlin, *North American Indians* (1841)

"At fifty yards a well-shapen, iron-pointed arrow is dangerous and very sure. A handful drawn from the quiver and discharged successively will make a more rapid fire than that of the revolver, and at very short range will farther penetrate a piece of plank or timber than the ball of an ordinary Colt's navy pistol."

Margaret I. Carrington, *Absaraka Home of the Crows* (1868)

The Surround
BY ALFRED JACOB MILLER. About 1850-60

"The plan of attack, which in this country is familiarly called a 'surround,' was explicitly agreed upon, and the hunters who were all mounted on their 'buffalo horses' and armed with bows and arrows or long lances, divided into two columns, taking opposite directions, and drew themselves gradually around the herd at a mile or more distance from them; thus forming a circle of horsemen at equal distances apart, who gradually closed in upon them with a moderate pace, at a signal given. The unsuspecting herd at length 'got the wind' of the approaching enemy and fled in a mass in the greatest confusion. To the point where they were aiming to cross the line, the horsemen were seen at full speed, gathering and forming in a column, brandishing their weapons and yelling in the most frightful manner, by which means they turned the black and rushing mass which moved off in an opposite direction where they were again met and foiled in a similar manner, and wheeled back in utter confusion; by which time the horsemen had closed in from all directions, forming a continuous line around them, whilst the poor affrighted animals were eddying about in a crowded and confused mass, hooking and climbing upon each other; when the work of death commenced."

George Catlin, *North American Indians* (1841)

Wenona's Leap
By Seth Eastman. About 1845

"Among all the modes of progression hitherto invented by restless man, there is not one that can compare in respect of comfort and luxury with travelling in a birchbark canoe. It is the poetry of progression. Along the bottom of the boat are laid blankets and bedding; a sort of wicker-work screen is sloped against the middle thwart, affording a delicious support to the back; and indolently, in your shirt sleeves if the day be warm, or well covered with a blanket if it is chilly, you sit or lie on this most luxurious of couches, and are propelled at a rapid rate over the smooth surface of a lake or down the swift current of some stream. If you want exercise, you can take a paddle yourself. If you prefer to be inactive, you can lie still and placidly survey the scenery, rising occasionally to have a shot at a wild duck; at intervals reading, smoking, and sleeping. Sleep indeed you will enjoy most luxuriously, for the rapid bounding motion of the canoe as she leaps forward at every impulse of the crew, the sharp quick beat of the paddles on the water, and the roll of their shafts against the gunwale, with the continuous hiss and ripple of the stream cleft by the curving prow, combine to make a more soothing soporific than all the fabrications of poppy and mandragora that can be found in the pharmacopoeia of civilization."

The Earl of Dunraven, *The Great Divide* (1876)

Lacrosse Playing among the Sioux Indians   *(color plate)*   [72]
By Seth Eastman. 1852

"It is no uncommon occurrence for six or eight hundred or a thousand of these young men to engage in a game of ball, with five or six times that number of spectators, of men, women, and children, surrounding the ground, and looking on. And I pronounce such a scene, with its hundreds of Nature's most beautiful models, denuded, and painted of various colours, running and leaping into the air, in all the most extravagant and varied forms, in the desperate struggles for the ball, a school for the painter or sculptor, equal to any of those which ever inspired the hand of the artist in the Olympian games or the Roman forum.

" . . . The Sioux use but one stick, which is generally held in both hands, with a round hoop at the end, in which the ball is caught and thrown with wonderful tact; a much more difficult feat, I should think, than that of the Choctaws, who catch the ball between two sticks."

George Catlin, *North American Indians* (1841)

Indian Sugar Camp
By SETH EASTMAN. About 1845

" . . . food has been scarce, and the wan faces of the children light up at the preparations for the sugar feast.

"The time has come, . . . the women [are] hard at work. Cutting wood, collecting the sap, boiling and straining it, keeps them pretty busy, while the men smoke, and lounge, and talk politics. The leaves of the maple are just starting into life, while it may be the snow has not melted from the distant hill-top.

"They all love sugar, men, women, and children; and the present is a gala time with them. The children will look as plump again by the time the generous sap ceases to run.

"For some weeks previous they have been making vessels of birch bark, in which to collect the sap. They strain it through their blankets, or anything that is convenient, not being particularly neat in their operations. When the sugar is made, it is put up in small birch bark baskets: the Chippewas call these Mococks. The sugar has a dark look, but a very pleasant flavor, provided they have not boiled it in the same kettle in which they cook their fish, which is too often the case."

Mary H. Eastman, *The American Aboriginal Portfolio* (1853)

[74]

Indians Travelling
BY SETH EASTMAN. About 1845

"As the population presses first on the Indian's hunting-grounds, and next on his cornfields, he flies before the irresistible tide, and takes shelter at some more remote western point. But he is hardly well seated on his new hunting-grounds—he has hardly begun to reap his new cornfields—when the pioneers of the same race that disturbed him before, are upon him; and again, and again he must fly before the resistless—the uncontrollable tide of migration."

Henry R. Schoolcraft, *Scenes and Adventures in the Semi-Alpine Region* (1853)

[75]

Dacota Encampment
BY SETH EASTMAN. About 1845

"A traveler in Indian country during the summer season cannot fail to be struck with the taste of the Indians as regards the location of their villages. Even if it be a mere encampment on a hunting excursion, the point of resting is sure to be where all that is attractive in nature meets the eye.

"The Indians must be near the river; and large trees must shade their buffalo tents. Convenience is not much consulted by the men, for they have only to eat, and lounge, and talk, when they are at home, the women having all else in their department. They make the lodges of buffalo-skin, always; for there is a tradition that one of their ancestors made hers of deer-skin, and died soon afterwards. This, to their superstitious minds, was an intimation that deer-skin was never more to be used for houses, for ever.

"The Dacota woman not only sews the buffalo-skin together, thus making her house, but, when on a journey, she carried it on her back. Long and weary may have been the day's travel; but she must put the stakes in the ground, and cover them with the buffalo-skins, then cut the wood to make the fire, and cook for the family before she rests."

Mary H. Eastman, *The American Aboriginal Portfolio* (1853)

[76]

Dacota Village
BY SETH EASTMAN. About 1845

"The summer houses of the Dacotas are made of the bark peeled from trees. The building of the house is the work of the women.

"These houses are quite comfortable, and their interiors are furnished with all that an Indian family deems necessary. Here they live, enjoying the warm weather, and preparing for the long, cold winter that will follow.

"They dry their skins on the scaffold attached to the house, making clothing of them when needed. Their corn may be seen hanging about, tied in bundles to dry, while all the other items of housewifery receive due attention.

"For these houses the bark of the elm tree is principally used. There is a quantity of this sort in the Sioux country. In the spring, the bark peels off easily in large pieces. The women have only to plant poles in the ground, fasten the bark to them, and the summer house is soon made. In the roof there is a hole cut that answers the purposes of a chimney. The fire in a Sioux or Dacota lodge is always kindled in the centre. A place in the lodge is allotted to each member of the family. The wife has hers near the door; being servant as well as wife, she is by custom placed where she can conveniently go in and out. The husband has his place near the fire."

Mary H. Eastman, *The American Aboriginal Portfolio* (1853)

[77]

An Osage Scalp Dance
By John Mix Stanley. 1845

"The nature of the outrages and barbarities perpetrated by these savages is not, I think, generally understood in the East. Murder and scalping are their mildest features. Their treatment of women and young girls beggars description. I was in Minnesota during the dreadful Sioux outbreak of 1862, and I speak within bounds in saying that is is impossible to write in English a description of the horrors inflicted on women. A man face to face with another man, would find it difficult to tell them! Language cannot render them."

J. F. Meline, *Two Thousand Miles on Horseback* (1867)

[78]

Prairie Indian Encampment
By John Mix Stanley. About 1845

"It needs but little familiarity with the actual, palpable aborigines to convince any one that the poetic Indian—the Indian of Cooper and Longfellow—is only visible to the poet's eye. To the prosaic observer, the average Indian of the woods and prairies is a being who does little credit to human nature—a slave of appetite and sloth, never emancipated from the tyranny of one animal passion save by the more ravenous demands of another. As I passed over those magnificent bottoms of the Kansas which form the reservations of the Delawares, Potawatamies, etc., constituting the very best corn-lands on earth, and saw their owners sitting around the doors of their lodges at the height of the planting season and in as good, bright planting weather as sun and soil ever made, I could not help saying, 'These people must die out—there is no help for them. God has given this earth to those who will subdue and cultivate it, and it is vain to struggle against His righteous decree.'"

Horace Greeley, *An Overland Journey, from New York to San Francisco* (1860)

[79]

Chinook Burial Grounds
By John Mix Stanley. Before 1860

"The body, instead of being consigned to mother earth, was placed on top of the platform. The latter was constructed of saplings, and was about twenty feet in height. From Comstock I learned that with some of the tribes this is the usual mode of disposing of the body after death. The prevailing belief of the Indian is that when done with this world the spirit of the deceased is transferred to the happy hunting-ground, where he is permitted to engage in the same pleasures and pursuits which he preferred while on earth. To this end it is deemed essential that after death the departed must be supplied with the same equipment and ornaments considered necessary while in the flesh. In accordance with this belief a complete Indian outfit, depending in extent upon the rank and importance of the deceased, is prepared, and consigned with the body to the final resting-place."

George A. Custer, *My Life on the Plains* (1874)

[30]

Indian Telegraph
By John Mix Stanley. 1860

"The transparency of the atmosphere upon the Plains is such that objects can be seen at great distances; a mountain, for example, presents a distinct and bold outline at fifty or sixty miles, and may occasionally be seen as far as a hundred miles.

"The Indians, availing themselves of this fact, have been in the habit of practicing a system of telegraphing by means of smokes during the day and fires by night, and, I dare say, there are but few travelers who have crossed the mountains to California that have not seen these signals made and responded to from peak to peak in rapid succession.

"The Indians thus make known to their friends many items of information highly important to them. If enemies or strangers make their appearance in the country, the fact is telegraphed at once, giving them time to secure their animals, and to prepare for attack, defense, or flight . . . "

Randolph B. Marcy, *Thirty Years of Army Life on the Border* (1866)

Assiniboin Encampment on the Upper Missouri
By JOHN MIX STANLEY. About 1860

"(Teepees or Tipi (French pron.?) belonging to Indians of the plains are sometimes forty feet in diam[e]t[e]r. The poles of tamarak are of large size to the protruding end of the tallest of which is suspended a horses tail as indicating the residence of a principal warrior or a chief, the exterior being decorated with diagrams of his principal actions. I know not why, but there is a *home* feeling about the interior of a teepee. As I have lounged on a buffalo robe by the light of a smouldering fire, it reminds me of my childish positions on the parlour rug in front of a hickory fire, during the winter evenings. The teepee is rendered very comfortable in the winter by piling straw around the exterior and strewing it within, & laying buffalo robes & furs upon it. Without, the snow accumulates above the straw leaving only the upper portion of the tent visible. Closing the entrance & building a fire it becomes a snug refuge from the inclement winters. Tepees last four or five years, but owing to the rotting of the lower portion of the skins decrease in size."

Frank Blackwell Mayer, *With Pen and Pencil on the Frontier in 1851*, edited by Bertha L. Heilbron, 1932

The Concealed Enemy
BY GEORGE CALEB BINGHAM. About 1850

"When an Indian sentinel intends to watch for an enemy approaching from the rear, he selects the highest position available, and places himself near the summit in such an attitude that his entire body shall be concealed from the observation of any one in the rear, his head only being exposed above the top of the eminence. Here he awaits with great patience so long as he thinks there is any possibility of danger, and it will be difficult for an enemy to surprise him or to elude his keen and scrutinizing vigilance. Meanwhile his horse is secured under the screen of the hill, all ready when required. Hence it will be evident that, in following Indian depredators, the utmost vigilance and caution must be exercised to conceal from them the movements of their pursuers. They are the best scouts in the world, proficient in all the artifices and stratagems available in border warfare, and when hotly pursued by a superior force, after exhausting all other means of evasion, they scatter in different directions; and if, in a broken or mountainous country, they can do no better, abandon their horses and baggage, and take refuge in the rocks, gorges, or other hiding-places."

Randolph B. Marcy, *Thirty Years of Army Life on the Border* (1866)

Indian Camp Fire
By CHARLES WIMAR. 1852

"In the course of my journey along the frontier, I have had repeated opportunities of noticing their excitability and boisterous merriment at their games;
and have occasionally noticed a group of Osages sitting round a fire until a
late hour of the night, engaged in the most animated and lively conversation;
and at times making the woods resound with peals of laughter. As to tears,
they have them in abundance, both real and affected; at times they make a
merit of them. No one weeps more bitterly or profusely at the death of a
relative or friend; and they have stated times when they repair to howl and
lament at their graves. I have heard doleful wailings at daybreak, in the neighboring Indian villages, made by some of the inhabitants, who go out at that
hour into the fields, to mourn and weep for the dead: at such times, I am told,
the tears will stream down their cheeks in torrents."

Washington Irving, *A Tour on the Prairies* (1835)

[84]

The Captive Charger
BY CHARLES WIMAR. 1854

"The wealth of an Indian consists chiefly in horses. Their horses come from Mexico, and are of as hardy stock as the Indians themselves. Whoever owns no horses tries to steal some. All stealing is permissible among the Indians, but horse-stealing is honorable. Such bands of horse thieves will often follow another tribe or a caravan of whites for weeks and months, till they find an opportunity to drive off the whole herd."

F. A. Wislizenus, *A Journey to the Rocky Mountains in the Year 1839* (1912)

[85]

Medicine Bag

BY CHARLES WIMAR. About 1858

"The word medicine, in its common acceptation here, means *mystery*, and nothing else; and in that sense I shall use it . . . in my notes on Indian manners and customs . . . The 'medicine-bag' then, is a mystery-bag; and its meaning and importance necessary to be understood, as it may be said to be the key of Indian life and Indian character. These bags are constructed of the skins of animals, of birds, or of reptiles, and ornamented and preserved in a thousand different ways, as suits the taste or freak of the person who constructs them. These skins are generally attached to some part of the clothing of the Indian, or carried in his hand—they are oftentimes decorated in such a manner as to be exceedingly ornamental to his person, and always are stuffed with grass, or moss, or something of the kind; and generally without drugs or medicines within them, as they are religiously closed and sealed, and seldom, if ever, to be opened. I find that every Indian in his primitive state, carries his medicine-bag in some form or other, to which he pays the greatest homage, and to which he looks for safety and protection through life—and in fact, it might almost be called a species of idolatry; for it would seem in some instances, as if he actually worshipped it."

George Catlin, *North American Indians* (1841)

Indians Approaching Fort Benton
BY CHARLES WIMAR. 1859

"While we were stopping around noon, we saw a band of Indians on the heights outlined against the sky. Since they had their baggage, their families, and their tents with them, it is evident that they were not on the warpath."

Philippe Regis de Trobriand, *Military Life in Dakota* (1867-1869), edited by Lucile M. Kane, 1951.

"The most attractive sight which we had yet met with upon this voyage, now presented itself to our view. The steam-boat lay too close to the willow thicket, and we saw, immediately before us, the numerous, motley, gaily painted, and variously ornamented crowd of the most elegant Indians on the whole course of the Missouri. The handsomest and most robust persons, of both sexes and all ages, in highly original, graceful, and characteristic costumes, appeared, thronged together, to our astonished eye; and there was, all at once, so much to see and observe, that we anxiously profited by every moment to catch only the main features of this unique picture. . . .

"All these Indians were dressed in their very finest clothes, and they completely attained their object; for they made, at least upon us strangers, a very lively impression. Many of them were distinguished by wearing leather shirts, of exquisite workmanship, which they obtain by barter from the Crows. Several tall, athletic men were on horseback, and managed their horses, which were frightened by the noise of the steam-boats, with an ease which afforded us pleasure."

Maximilian, Prince of Wied, *Travels in the Interior of North America* (1843)

[87]

The Buffalo Hunt
BY CHARLES WIMAR. 1860

"The chief hunting amusement of the Indians in these parts consists in the chase of buffalo, which is almost invariably done on horseback, with bow and lance. In this exercise, which is highly prized by them, as one of their most valued amusements, as well as for the principal mode of procuring meat for their subsistence, they become exceedingly expert; and are able to slay these huge animals with apparent ease.

"The Indians in these parts are all mounted on small, but serviceable horses, which are caught by them on the prairies, where they are often running wild in numerous bands. The Indian, then, mounted on his little wild horse, which has been through some years of training, dashes off at full speed amongst the herds of buffaloes, elks, or even antelopes, and deals his deadly arrows to their hearts from his horse's back. The horse is the fleetest animal of the prairie, and easily brings his rider alongside of his game, which falls a certain prey to his deadly shafts, at the distance of a few paces."

George Catlin, *North American Indians* (1841)

[120]

The Buffalo Dance   (*color plate*)

BY CHARLES WIMAR, 1860

"The place where this strange operation is carried on is in the public area in the centre of the village, and in front of the great medicine or mystery lodge. About ten or fifteen Mandans at a time join in the dance, each one with the skin of the buffalo's head (or mask) with the horns on, placed over his head, and in his hand his favourite bow or lance, with which he is used to slay the buffalo.

"I mentioned that this dance always had the desired effect, that it never fails, nor can it, for it cannot be stopped (but is going incessantly day and night) until 'buffalo come.' Drums are beating and rattles are shaken, and songs and yells incessantly are shouted, and lookers-on stand ready with masks on their heads, and weapons in hand, to take the place of each one as he becomes fatigued, and jumps out of the ring.

"These dances have sometimes been continued in this village two and three weeks without stopping an instant, until the joyful moment when buffaloes made their appearance."

George Catlin, *North American Indians* (1841)

[88]

[121]

[89]

The Last of the Buffalo   (*see frontispiece*)
By Albert Bierstadt. After 1858

"Reckless, moreover, of the future, in order to prepare robes for the traders, and produce the pernicious fire-water, they wantonly slaughter vast numbers of buffalo cows every year (the skins of which sex only are dressed), and thus add to the evils in store for them. When questioned on this subject, and such want of foresight being pointed out to them, they answer, that however quickly the buffalo disappears, the Red man 'goes under' in greater proportion; and that the Great Spirit has ordained that both shall be 'rubbed out' from the face of nature at one and the same time—'that arrows and bullets are not more fatal to the buffalo than the small-pox and fire-water to them, and that before many winters' snows have disappeared, the buffalo and the Red man will only be remembered by their bones, which will strew the plains.' "

George Frederick Ruxton, *Life in the Far West* (1849)

[90]

Indian Camp at Fort Laramie
By Frank Buchser. 1866

"Their tepee is the model from which the Sibley tent was derived, and will accommodate several families; but nothing else on the face of the earth will furnish a more curious medley of contents than does a tepee where two or three families, of all ages and sizes, with all their worldly goods and hopes are huddled, piled, and crammed about its fire, and where the fitful wind and lazy squaws are combined in the effort to smoke buffalo tongues, strips of meat, and *Injun* all together. The picture is complete, by way of contrast, if a kettle of boiling water over the fire has received a fat dog just after his throat felt the knife, and a white officer, on a pile of furs, is doing his best to show how gracefully he can endure the honors and dinner specially designed for his presence."

Margaret I. Carrington, *Absaraka Home of the Crows* (1868)

"The western Dakota have no fixed habitations. Hunting and fighting, they wander incessantly through summer and winter. Some are following the herds of buffalo over the waste of prairie; others are traversing the Black Hills, thronging on horseback and on foot through the dark gulfs and somber gorges beneath the vast splintering precipices, and emerging at last upon the 'Parks,' those beautiful but most perilous hunting grounds."

Francis Parkman, *The California and Oregon Trail* (1849)

*Sa-tan-ti Addressing the Peace Commissioners at Council Grove,
Medicine Lodge Creek, 1867*
BY HERMANN STIEFFEL. Probably 1879

"I regret to have to report that since August last up to the present time the
Cheyennes and Arapahoes of the plains have been on the warpath. Since I
have been Superintendent, I have indulged the hope that these Indians might,
by proper management and kind treatment on the part of the government, be
induced to abandon their wild and savage habits, and live at peace with the
whites. Their last outbreak compels me reluctantly to abandon this long
cherished hope. Heretofore when these Indians have made war, I felt that in a
measure they had cause. This time they had none. Since the treaty of Medicine
Lodge Creek, in the fall of 1867, these Indians have been well treated. Every
promise made them in the treaty by the Indian peace commissioners, (nay more,
for they were fed during the whole of last winter) has been strictly complied
with; yet as I before remarked, without provocation they attacked the white
settlers in the western portion of this state and committed deeds of rapine,
murder and other outrages too atrocious to be written."

Thomas Murphy, *Report of the Superintendent of Indian Affairs* (1868)

[92]

The Ambush
By Paul Frenzeny. 1883

"Their spies occupy the bluffs constantly, and as they have good field-glasses, which they purchase from the traders, they can distinguish every movement for twenty miles. It seems impossible to Eastern readers that they can so readily ascertain every movement; but when it is considered that a train can be seen distinctly on the plain ten miles distant with the naked eye, it needs no argument to prove that the Indians, with good glasses, know every military movement as soon as it is commenced."

A. K. McClure, *Three Thousand Miles through the Rocky Mountains* (1869)

"Old Major Bridger, in his peculiarly quaint and sensible way, dropped the sentiment: 'Better not go fur. There is Injuns enough lying under wolf skins, or skulking on them cliffs, I warrant! They follow ye always. They've seen ye, every day, and when ye don't see any of 'em about, is just the time to look out for their devilment.'"

Margaret I. Carrington, *Absaraka Home of the Crows* (1868)

The Scout: Friends or Enemies
By FREDERIC REMINGTON. About 1895

"Encountering people in these solitudes is like meeting a suspicious sail at sea when your country is at war, and you are uncertain as to the character, nationality, intentions, size, and strength of the stranger. The latter point is the most important to clear up. Man is the most dangerous beast that roams . . . , and the first idea that enters the mind on meeting him or seeing his traces is one of hostility; you take it for granted that he is an enemy and to be guarded against, until you ascertain that he is a friend and can be trusted."

The Earl of Dunraven, *The Great Divide* (1876)

The Birds and Animals

 THE WILD creatures of the West were second only to the Indians as compelling subject matter to the artist of the Louisiana Territory. One scarcely needed to hunt them out; they were encountered everywhere. There were the fur-bearing animals of the river banks that had first tempted the white man westward up the Missouri. There were the animals of the mountains and woodlands like the bighorn, the bear and the deer. There were the animals of the Plains, the antelope, the wolf and coyote, the ubiquitous little prairie dog, the jack rabbit, and the herds of wild horses. And there was the buffalo—fifteen million strong, according to one estimate. The woods were alive with countless birds, many of them still familiar, others that have disappeared like the flocks of parakeets and wild turkeys, the clouds of passenger pigeons and the whooping crane. The Plains supported the prairie chicken and the sage grouse amongst many others, the birds of prey and the scavengers like the red-tailed hawk, the turkey buzzard, the vulture and the carrion crow. The eagle, venerated by the Indians, inhabited the cliffs and mountains.

Surrounded by this prodigality of nature many of the artists who ventured beyond the Mississippi were moved to create some of the most beautiful and fascinating pictures of the western scene. The earliest of them was by far the greatest, John James Audubon. With good reason the largest part of this section of the book is given over to him.

An ornithologist from boyhood, Audubon first entered the new American Territory of Louisiana in January 1810 at St. Genevieve, Missouri and it was there, while still an unsuccessful merchant, that he must have painted the ivory-billed woodpecker, green heron, and red-tailed hawk that are dated in that year and that appear in the following pages. Promising as early efforts, they represent a prelude to the monumental achievement that began in earnest ten years later when he conceived his *Birds of America.* As Audubon himself expressed it: "Nothing . . . could ever answer my enthusiastic desires to represent nature, except to copy her in her own way, alive and moving!" In 1820 with New Orleans as a base he commenced work on his first great watercolors for the "elephant folio," while at the same time he scouted the lower valley for specimens. For six years he labored, then departed not to return until 1843 when he had begun his second vast project, *The Quadrupeds of North America,* which took him far up the Missouri as far as the Yellowstone in quest of the animals of the western waterways, plains and mountains. In this huge enterprise he was most ably assisted artistically by his son John Woodhouse Audubon whose work is here reproduced along with his father's.

John James Audubon was the only artist of the West who concerned himself seriously with birds, but others before him had painted pictures of western animals that do not suffer by comparison.

The earliest of them, Peter Rindisbacher, though by no means the artist Audubon was, has the distinction of being the first to paint the buffalo in his natural habitat. Probably as early as 1825 while not yet twenty, this young Swiss who had migrated with his parents to Lord Selkirk's Red River colony painted the buffalo grazing in winter and hunted by the Indians near the present border between North Dakota and Canada. Catlin painted the buffalo, the deer and the gray wolf in 1832. But a far more accomplished and sensitive artist than either of his predecessors, Charles Bodmer, focused his penetrating eye on the animals of the West the following year, producing the delicate watercolor details of sheep and antelope here published for the first time, and his beautiful aquatints composed from sketches made on the upper Missouri. Hardly less interesting, though less explicit in drawing, are the buffalo and wild steeds of the Indians that Alfred Jacob Miller painted on his tour of the West with Captain William Drummond Stewart in 1837.

Twenty years later Charles Wimar of St. Louis was taking his summer trips up the Missouri, and possibly up the Platte as well, in quest of material for his Indian paintings. To this absorbing interest, the buffalo was only second. Trained at Düsseldorf, he was habituated to making detail sketches in oil as well as in pencil and charcoal. His oil sketch of quartered buffalo is the only known rendering of this staple of Plains diet a century ago. Bierstadt with the same academic training also made numerous oil sketches beginning with his first excursion in the

West in 1858 when he probably painted the *Buffalo Bull* as reference for a later studio composition. Frank Buchser, the Swiss painter who in 1866 spent four months of his five years in America in the Far West was, like Wimar, attracted by an "animal still life" and painted the remarkable *Cadaver of an Ox*, a forlorn and common sight on the Plains. In 1860 William Jacob Hays of New York made the riverboat trip up the Missouri, an experience that furnished him with lasting material in building his reputation as an animal painter in the latter nineteenth century.

Green Heron [94]

Ivory-billed Woodpecker [95] *Red-tailed Hawk*

Three Birds of Missouri
BY J. J. AUDUBON. 1810

"I continued for months together, simply outlining birds as I observed them, either alighted or on the wing, but could finish none of my sketches. I procured many individuals of different species, and laying them on the table or on the ground, tried to place them in such attitudes as I had sketched. But, alas! they were dead, to all intents and purposes, and neither wing, leg, nor tail could I place according to my wishes. A second thought came to my assistance; by means of threads I raised or lowered a head, wing, or tail, and by fastening the threads securely, I had something like life before me; yet much was wanting. When I saw the living birds, I felt the blood rush to my temples, and almost in despair spent a month without drawing, but in deep thought, and daily in the company of the feathered inhabitants of dear Mill Grove. . . . I was off to the creek, and shot the first Kingfisher I met. I picked the bird up, carried it home by the bill, sent for the miller, and bade him bring me a piece of board of soft wood. When he returned he found me filing sharp points to some pieces of wire, and I proceeded to show him what I meant to do. I pierced the body of the fishing bird, and fixed it on the board; another wire passed above his upper mandible held the head in a pretty fair attitude, smaller ones fixed the feet according to my notions, and even common pins came to my assistance. The last wire proved a delightful elevator to the bird's tail, and at last—there stood before me the real Kingfisher. . . . This was what I shall call my first drawing actually from nature, for even the eye of the Kingfisher was as if full of life whenever I pressed the lids aside with my finger. . . .

"As I wandered, mostly bent on the study of birds, and with a wish to represent all those found in our woods, to the best of my powers, I gradually became acquainted with their forms and habits, and the use of my wires was improved by constant practice. Whenever I produced a better representation of any species the preceding one was destroyed, and after a time I laid down what I was pleased to call a constitution of my manner of drawing birds, formed upon natural principles, which I will try to put briefly before you. . . .

"My drawings at first were made altogether in watercolors, but they wanted softness and a great deal of finish. For a long time I was much dispirited at this, particularly when vainly endeavoring to imitate birds of soft and downy plumage, such as that of most Owls, Pigeons, Hawks, and Herons. How this could be remedied required a new train of thought, or some so-called accident and the latter came to my aid. . . .

"My drawings of Owls and other birds of similar plumage were much improved by such applications; indeed, after a few years of patience, some of my attempts began almost to please me, and I have continued the same style ever since, and that now if for more than thirty years."

Maria R. Audubon, editor, *Audubon and His Journals* (1897)

[97]

Wild Turkey Cock
ENGRAVING AFTER A DRAWING BY J. J. AUDUBON. 1826-27

"Turkey, *meleagris gallipavo*. The wild turkey is a fine, large bird, of brilliant, blackish plumage. It breeds with the domestic one; and when the latter is reared near the range of the former, it is sure to be enticed into the woods by it. In some places they are so numerous, as to be easily killed, beyond the wants of the people. We have seen more than an hundred driven from one corn field. The Indians, and the western sportsmen, learn a way to hunt them, by imitating the cry of their young."

Timothy Flint, *The History and Geography of the Mississippi Valley* (1831)

"Scarcely had we dismounted, when a universal firing of rifles took place upon a large flock of turkeys, scattered about the grove, which proved to be a favorite roosting-place for these simple birds. They flew to the trees, and sat perched upon their branches, stretching out their long necks, and gazing in stupid astonishment, until eighteen of them were shot down."

Washington Irving, *A Tour on the Prairies* (1835)

[98]

Whooping Crane
ENGRAVING AFTER A DRAWING BY J. J. AUDUBON. 1834

". . . between Muscleshell and Milk Rivers, we passed the Half-way Pyramid which lay to the south of us. During the whole day we saw many buffaloes and elks, and a skunk on the bank, which escaped us, and a small flock of the hooping crane, one of the finest birds of North America, which was on its flight to warmer regions. . . .

"We soon came to the rude, apparently desolate chain of hills that extends to Fort Union, proceeded till one o'clock in the morning, and then, cold and benumbed, lay to at a sand bank, when those especially whose turn it was to keep watch had no very enviable lot. Cranes awoke at the same time as we did early in the morning of the 29th, and rose with loud cries in the misty air."

Maximilian, Prince of Wied, *Travels in the Interior of North America* (1843)

[99]

Barn Owl
Engraving after a drawing by J. J. Audubon. 1833

"A great many varieties of this bird are found here. Their hooting and scream-ing, in every variety of tone and sound, often imitating the cry of human distress and laughter, and sometimes the shrieks of a babe, are heard over all this valley in the deep forests and bottoms."

Timothy Flint, *The History and Geography of the Mississippi Valley* (1831)

[100]

Turkey Buzzard
Engraving after a drawing by J. J. Audubon. 1832

"A great flock of Buzzards were usually soaring about a few trees that stood on the island just below our camp. Throughout the whole of yesterday we had noticed an eagle among them; to-day he was still there; and Tete Rouge, declaring that he would kill the bird of America, borrowed Delorier's gun and set out on his unpatriotic mission. As might have been expected, the eagle suffered no great harm at his hands. He soon returned, saying that he could not find him, but had shot a buzzard instead. . . .

". . . The air above this spot was always full of buzzards or black vultures. . . . These birds would now be sailing by scores just above our camp, their broad black wings seeming half transparent as they expanded them against the bright sky. The wolves and the buzzards thickened about us with every hour, and two or three eagles also came into the feast."

Francis Parkman, *The California and Oregon Trail* (1849)

[101]

Pinnated Grouse or Prairie Chicken
ENGRAVING AFTER A DRAWING BY J. J. AUDUBON. 1834

"And we have birds to enliven our progress. The road is alive with the mule-bird, whip-poor-will, doves, plover, and meadow lark. Of grouse, or prairie chicken, we have scared up a dozen or two. They are, of course, more shy than the others, but off the road and out in the prairie the hunter would, doubtless, find them more abundant. I speak of Kansas, for we have not seen one in Nebraska."

J. F. Meline, *Two Thousand Miles on Horseback* (1867)

"In these delightful amusements, and with these pleasing companions, I have been for a while participating with great satisfaction; I have joined several times in the deer-hunts, and more frequently in grouse shooting, which constitutes the principal amusement of this place.

"This delicious bird, which is found in great abundance in nearly all the North American prairies, and most generally called the Prairie Hen, is, from what I can learn, very much like the English grouse, or heath hen, both in size, in colour, and in habits. They make their appearance in these parts in the months of August and September, from the higher latitudes, where they go in the early part of the summer, to raise their broods. This is the season for the best sport amongst them; and the whole garrison, in fact, are almost subsisted on them at this time, owing to the facility with which they are killed."

George Catlin, *North American Indians* (1841)

[102]

Cock of the Plains or Sage Grouse
ENGRAVING AFTER A DRAWING BY J. J. AUDUBON. 1837

"The most serious cause of regret that I feel for my present inefficient condition of the body, is the being unable to accompany Bell and Owen McKenzie who have set out this morning on horseback to go two days journey up the Yellowstone in search of the Cock of the Plains, which, or birds very similar, were seen by Owen about two weeks ago on his return from carrying an express to Mr. Kipp on his way to Fort Alexander, the Crow station. As a sportsman the shooting of this bird is the height of my ambition, and I am now compelled to abandon forever the idea of killing one."

Up the Missouri with Audubon. The Journal of Edward Harris (1843), edited by John Francis McDermott, 1951

[103]

Carolina Parrot or Parakeet
ENGRAVING AFTER A DRAWING BY J. J. AUDUBON. About 1830

"Gérard was all curiosity to see my drawings, and old Redouté, who was present, spoke so highly of them before the book was opened, that I feared to discover Gérard's disappointment. The book opened accidentally at the plate of the Parrots, and Gérard, taking it up without speaking, looked at it, I assure thee, with as keen an eye as my own, for several minutes; put it down, took up the one of the Mocking-Birds, and, offering me his hand, said: 'Mr. Audubon, you are the king of ornithological painters; we are all children in France and in Europe. Who would have expected such things from the woods of America?'"

Maria R. Audubon, editor, *Audubon and his Journals* (1897)

[104]

Buffaloes in Winter
By Peter Rindisbacher. About 1825

"It is very evident that, as high North as Lake Winnipeg, seven or eight hundred miles North of this, the buffalo subsists itself through the severest winters: getting its food chiefly by browsing amongst the timber, and by pawing through the snow, for a bite at the grass, which in those regions is frozen up very suddenly in the beginning of the winter, with all its juices in it, and consequently furnishes very nutritious and efficient food."

George Catlin, *North American Indians* (1841)

[105]

Head of a Bighorn Calf
BY CHARLES BODMER. 1833

"In some places there are piles of earth from eight to ten feet high, or even more, the tops of which form platforms of a hard and shelly rocky substance, where the Bighorn is often seen looking on the hunter far below, and standing immovable, as if a statue. No one can imagine how they reach these places, and that too with their young, even when the latter are quite small. Hunters say that the young are usually born in such places, the mothers going there to save the helpless little one from the Wolves, which, after men, seem to be their greatest destroyers. The Mauvaises Terres are mostly formed of grayish white clay, very sparsely covered with small patches of thin grass, on which the Bighorns feed, but which, to all appearance, is a very scanty supply, and there, and there only, they feed, as not one has ever been seen on the bottom or prairie land further than the foot of these most extraordinary hills. In wet weather, no man can climb any of them, and at such times they are greasy, muddy, sliding grounds. Oftentimes when a Bighorn is seen on a hill-top, the hunter has to ramble about for three or four miles before he can approach within gunshot of the game, and if the Bighorn ever sees his enemy, pursuit is useless."

Maria R. Audubon, editor, *Audubon and His Journals* (1897)

[106]

Head of a Prong-horned Antelope Calf
BY CHARLES BODMER. 1833

"The antelope of this country, I believe to be different from all other known varieties, and forms one of the most pleasing, living ornaments to this western world. They are seen in some places in great numbers sporting and playing about the hills and dales; and often, in flocks of fifty or a hundred, will follow the boat of the descending voyageur, or the travelling caravan, for hours together; keeping off at a safe distance, on the right or left, galloping up and down the hills, snuffing their noses and stamping their feet. . . .

"This little animal seems to be endowed, like many other gentle and sweet breathing creatures, with an undue share of curiosity, which often leads them to destruction; and the hunter who wishes to entrap them, saves himself the trouble of travelling after them. When he has been discovered, he has only to elevate above the tops of the grass, his red or yellow handkerchief on the end of his gun-rod, which he sticks in the ground, and to which they are sure to advance, though with great coyness and caution; whilst he lies close, at a little distance, with his rifle in hand. . . ."

George Catlin, *North American Indians* (1841)

[141]

Beaver Hut on the Missouri

AQUATINT AFTER A DRAWING BY CHARLES BODMER. 1839

"The beaver is about two feet long, has a thick heavy body, compressed head with short elliptical ears, and somewhat oval, but rather broad tail, about ten inches long and covered with scales. The whole body is covered with a dense fur, consisting of longer reddish brown and shorter silvery hair. The skill of these animals in constructing their dwellings is well known. They prefer living on brooks and streamlets whose shores are overgrown with willows. In order to have deep water continually, they build a dam through the water, sometimes diagonally, sometimes in a convex bow. At this dam all the colony of beavers living together work jointly. Their only tools for this building are their teeth, their claws and their tail. In the water thus dammed up, each beaver family builds for itself out of the same material little square dwellings. . . . Their dwellings, which they frequently repair, become in time so firm that they can only be broken with tools. The greater part of these dwellings is under water; but there is under the roof a space without water, as the beavers cannot remain long under water without breathing. The conical roof is often four to six feet thick. The interior of their dwellings they keep very neat. Every dwelling has, deep down in the water, on the side furthest removed from the shore, an opening for the entrance and exit of its inmates. Beavers work only at night. By day they do not leave their dams, and swim, when going from one cone to another, so far under water that one cannot notice them."

F. A. Wislizenus, *A Journey to the Rocky Mountains in the Year 1839* (1912)

Scenting the Breeze
By Alfred Jacob Miller. 1837

"In putting off from a bluff on the S. W. side, to cross over, my attention was called to an object which attracted the notice of the company. A huge buffaloe bull made his appearance on the top of the bluff standing almost at the edge of the precipice, and looking down upon us. It was the first we had seen. Long and matted wool hung over his head, and covered his huge shoulders, while his body was smooth, as also the tail, except a tuft at the end. It was a striking and terrific object: he eyed us with the ferocity of the lion, seemed at length to 'snuff the tainted breeze:' threw his head into the air, wheeled round and trotted off. It was fifteen minutes before he disappeared entirely, and I continued to follow him with my eyes, with a kind of delight. I was told he had gone to join his comrade; the males at this season of the year always go in pairs, a singular fact in the natural history of the animal."

H. M. Brackenridge, *Journal of a Voyage up the River Missouri in 1811* (1814)

[109]

Buffaloes Drinking and Bathing at Night
BY ALFRED JACOB MILLER. 1837

"Two things are essential to the well-being and comfort of this animal—he must have his water bath, which he usually takes at night, and his earth bath, with which he solaces himself during the day . . . The scene of the sketch is on the Platte,—at night the Buffaloes come to the River banks in legions, to quench thirst and refresh themselves by swimming. Luckily for them they are rarely disturbed at this hour."

Alfred Jacob Miller, *Notes* (1837) quoted in *The West of Alfred Jacob Miller,* edited by Marvin C. Ross, 1951

Black-tailed Hare or Jack Rabbit
By J. J. Audubon. 1841

" 'I chanced to to be visited by some of the Shawnee Indians who were in the neighbourhood on a hunting expedition. They were highly astonished and pleased with my drawings, which I exhibited to them while trying to explain what animals I wanted. I made a hasty sketch of a hare with immensely long ears, at which I pointed with an approving nod of the head, and then made another sketch smaller and with shorter ears, at which last I shook my head and made wry faces; the Indians laughed, and by their gutteral eugh, haugh, li, gave me to understand that they comprehend me; and in a day or two, I had a beautiful specimen of the Black-tailed Hare brought to me.' . . . This species is called the *Jackass Rabbit* in Texas, owing to the length of its ears."

J. J. Audubon and John Bachman, *The Quadrupeds of North America* (1849)

" . . . we had proceeded only a short distance when a large jack-rabbit hopped out from among the willows, straightening himself up as if taking in the situation. Our anxiety and imagination, re-inforced by our empty stomachs, made that jack-rabbit look to be three or four feet high. Without the least hesitation, I think we made what modern hunters would call a pot-shot, but we got the rabbit. Returning to camp with our prize, we soon had choice cuts of rabbit cooking from the end of willow sticks. . . . Steve declared that 'he who had never eaten broiled jack-rabbit, seasoned with salt, knew very little about good living.' "

Reuben Cole Shaw, *Across the Plains in Forty-nine* (1896)

Fisher or Marten
By J. J. Audubon. About 1840

"On our arrival at the place, it was already light, and the dogs were barking furiously at the foot of the tree. We soon perceived that instead of being a racoon, the animal was a far more rare and interesting species, a Fisher. As we were anxious to study its habits we did not immediately shoot, but teased it by shaking some grape vines that had crept up nearly to the top of the tree. The animal not only became thoroughly frightened but seemed furious; he leaped from branch to branch, showing his teeth and growling at the same time; now and then he ran half way down the trunk of the tree, elevating his back in the manner of an angry cat, and we every moment expected to see him leap off and fall among the dogs. He was brought down after several discharges from the gun. He seemed extremely tenacious of life, and was game to the last, holding on to the nose of a dog with a dying grasp."

J. J. Audubon and John Bachman, *The Quadrupeds of North America* (1849)

Wolverene
By J. J. Audubon. About 1840

"It has been asserted that the Wolverene is a great destroyer of beavers, but we are inclined to think that this can scarcely be the case, unless it be in summer, when the beaver is often found some distance from the water. In such cases we presume that the Wolverene, although not swift of foot, could easily overtake that aquatic animal. But, should he in winter attempt to break open the frozen mud-walls of the beaver-huts, which would be a very difficult task, this would only have the effect of driving the occupants into their natural element, the water, where their hungry pursuer could not follow them. The statement of his expertness in swimming, diving, and catching fish, we believe to be apocryphal. . . .

"That it seizes on deer or large game by pouncing on them is incredible; it neither possesses the agility nor the strength to accomplish this feat. This habit has also been ascribed to the Canada lynx as well as to the Bay lynx; we do not think it applies to either. That the Wolverene occasionally captures the grouse that have plunged into the fresh snow as a protection from the cold is probable. Richardson observes that he saw one chasing an American hare, which was at the same time harassed by a snowy owl. The speed of the hare however is such that it has not much to fear from the persevering but slow progress of the Wolverene; and the one seen by Richardson, in his efforts to catch the tempting game must have been prompted by a longing desire after hare's flesh, rather than by any confidence in his ability to overtake the animal."

J. J. Audubon and John Bachman, *The Quadrupeds of North America* (1849)

[113]

Say's or Western Fox Squirrel
By J. J. Audubon. 1843

"It is a cheering spectacle in autumn, to walk in the beech and hickory bottoms, where you may often see, at one view, half a dozen of these active and proud little animals, flourishing their erect and spread tails, barking defiance at you, or each other, and skipping, as if by the aid of wings, from branch to branch. It is a fact, to which we can bear ocular testimony, that they cross rivers; at some times swimming; at other times on a chip, or piece of bark, raising and spreading their tails, by way of sail. It often happens to these, as to other inexperienced navigators, that they spread too much canvass, and are overset, and drowned. It is related, as having happened in the year 1811, that they emigrated from the north towards the south by thousands, and with a front of some regularity . . ."

Timothy Flint, *The History and Geography of the Mississippi Valley* (1831)

Head of a Buffalo Calf
By J. J. Audubon. 1843

"The buffalo calf, during the first six months is red, and has so much the appearance of a red calf in cultivated fields, that it could easily be mingled and mistaken amongst them. In the fall, when it changes its hair, it takes a brown coat for the winter, which it always retains. In pursuing a large herd of buffaloes at the season when their calves are but a few weeks old, I have often been exceedingly amused with the curious manoeuvres of these shy little things. Amidst the thundering confusion of a throng of several hundreds or several thousands of these animals, there will be many of the calves that lose sight of their dams; and being left behind by the throng, and the swift passing hunters, they endeavour to secrete themselves, when they are exceedingly put to it on a level prairie, where nought can be seen but the short grass of six or eight inches in height, save an occasional bunch of wild sage, a few inches higher, to which the poor affrighted things will run, and dropping on their knees, will push their noses under it, and into the grass, where they will stand for hours, with their eyes shut, imagining themselves securely hid, whilst they are standing up quite straight upon their hind feet, and can easily be seen at several miles distance."

George Catlin, *North American Indians* (1841)

[115]

Leopard Ground-Squirrel or Chipmunk
LITHOGRAPH AFTER A DRAWING BY J. J. AUDUBON. 1844

"In the warm days of spring the traveller on our Western prairies is often diverted from the contemplation of larger animals, to watch the movements of this lively little species. He withdraws his attention for a moment from the bellowing buffalo herd that is scampering over the prairies, to fix his eyes on a lively little creature of exquisite beauty seated on a diminutive mound at the mouth of its burrow, which seems by its chirrupings and scoldings to warn away the intruder on its peaceful domains. On a nearer approach it darts into its hole; but although concealed from view, and out of the reach of danger, its tongue, like that of other scolds of a more intelligent race, is not idle; it still continues to vent its threats of resentment against its unwelcome visitor by a shrill and harsh repetition of the 'seek-seek'. . . .

"As soon as they feel the warmth of spring they come forth and go in quest of their mates; at this period they seem fearless of danger, and are easily captured by the beasts and birds of prey that frequent the plains. The males are said to be very pugnacious at this season. . . .

"We found the Leopard-Spermophile quite abundant near Fort Union, on the Upper Missouri. Their burrows were made in a sandy gravelly soil, they were never deep or inclined downwards, but ran horizontally within about a foot of the surface of the earth."

J. J. Audubon and John Bachman, *The Quadrupeds of North America* (1849)

[116]

Prairie Dogs
LITHOGRAPH AFTER A DRAWING BY J. J. AUDUBON. 1846

". . . my objection to prairie-dog is a radical one, to wit: he is no dog at all. He has nothing in common with the dog. He is of the rodentia family, has the head, jaws and teeth, nails and body of a squirrel; sits up on his haunches as the squirrel does, and handles and nibbles his food in the same manner. His bark is not a bark, but more like the chirrup of a bird, or the 'cheep', 'cheep', of a ground-squirrel. I at first listened to it for a day or two without dreaming it came from a quadruped. In shape, form, and action he more nearly resembles the chipmunk, or ground-squirrel, than any animal I know, and is twice or thrice its size. His color is a light, dirty, reddish brown. All the feet are five toed and provided with long black nails, the thumb being armed with a strong conic nail three tenths of an inch in length. I measured three of them, who were, respectively, fifteen, fifteen and a half, and sixteen inches in length. When caught young he is easily tamed, and will follow you about like a playful kitten—I say when caught, for the catching is not easy. It is useless to shoot at them for that purpose, as, if wounded, they always contrive to get into their holes. Hence a popular prairie fiction, that, in such cases, they are always hauled in by their companions. Drowning out is a method of getting at them greatly in vogue—not always successful, for I have seen several barrels of water used without effect."

J. F. Meline, *Two Thousand Miles on Horseback* (1867)

[151]

[117]

Prong-horned Antelope
By J. W. Audubon. 1843

"This is the most swift and beautiful little animal on our continent. The description of the gazel of Africa, the favorite theme of Arabian poetry, might be applied to the antelope of the Missouri. It is perhaps, the most swift of all animals; and the most timid. Its course over the country is more like flight, than the movement of a quadruped. Its color is that of the deer, but in shape it bears a greater resemblance to the goat, though larger, and of a form much more delicate; I often amuse myself with watching the motions of this little animal."

H. M. Brackenridge, *Journal of a Voyage up the River Missouri in 1811* (1814)

"In some valleys near the Rocky Mountains, where the pasturage is good during the winter season, they collect in immense herds. The Indians are in the habit of surrounding them in such localities and running them with their horses until they tire them out, then they slay large numbers."

Randolph B. Marcy, *The Prairie Traveler* (1863)

Common American Deer
By J. W. AUDUBON. 1843

"We halted in the shade of the rock wall, and, while deeply interested in surrounding objects, were startled by a peculiar rushing sound from up the creek which seemed to be drawing nearer. We first thought of mounted Indians, but before we had time to take the second thought six deer, with a very large buck in the lead, were within fifty feet of us, with nothing intervening except low, scrubby bushes. On seeing us they changed their course and started up the opposite slope, when our four guns, heavily charged with buckshot, were all fired at once, and the old buck came tumbling down the steep bank almost to our feet, while we were surprised and dumbfounded at seeing the other five deer scamper off up the hill quite unhurt. In dressing the game we noticed that its hide was completely riddled with buckshot, and on consulting together we found that in our hurry and excitement all had fired at that tough old buck and let the young and tender meat go scot-free."

Reuben Cole Shaw, *Across the Plains in Forty-nine* (1896)

Black-tailed Deer

Lithograph after a drawing by J. J. Audubon. 1845

"When on the Upper Missouri, near Fort Union, we obtained through the aid of our hunters, the female Black-tailed Deer, from which our figure, description and measurements have been made. We regret exceedingly that we were so unfortunate as not to have been able to procure a male, the delineation of which we must leave to our successors.

"The habits of this animal approach more nearly those of the Elk, than of either the long-tailed or Virginian Deer. Like the former they remove far from the settlements, fly from the vicinity of the hunter's camp, and when once fairly started, run for a mile or two before they come to a pause.

"The female produces one or two young, in the month of June.

"We have figured a female in summer pelage, and have represented the animal in an exhausted state, wounded through the body, and about to drop down, whilst the hunter is seen approaching, through the tall grass, anticipating the moment when she will reel and fall in her tracks."

J. J. Audubon and John Bachman, *The Quadrupeds of North America* (1849)

Prairie Wolf or Coyote
BY J. W. AUDUBON. 1843

"The prairie-wolf was the first of these gentry to pay his respects to us. He is a sneaking, cowardly little wretch, of a dull or dirty white color, much resembling a small, short-bodied dog set up on pretty long legs. I believe his only feat entitling him to rank as a beast of prey consists in sometimes, when hard pressed by hunger, digging out a prairie-dog and making a meal of him. His usual provender is the carcass—no matter how putrid—of any dead buffalo, mule, or ox that he may find exposed on the prairie. He is a paltry creature."

Horace Greeley, *Overland Journey, from New York to San Francisco* (1860)

"The prairie wolf is of a lighter gray, . . . They have sharp(er) noses, and a form more resembling that of a fox. They are cold, fierce, cunning and mischievous animals, and, in their bark and howl, not easily distinguished from the domestic dog. They sometimes travel in packs on the prairies. We have often heard their shrill and sharp bark by night, from a cabin on the prairies. It was evidently a note of defiance to the dogs of the house. The latter retreat towards the cabin, evidencing fear, and diminishing their bark to a whine, and finally pawing at the door for admission within. They are a most annoying scourge to the farmer, and, in fact, the greatest impediment to the raising of sheep on the prairies."

Timothy Flint, *The History and Geography of the Mississippi Valley* (1831)

[121]

Gray Wolf or White American Wolf
By J. W. AUDUBON. 1843

"But the gray-wolf—who is also a denizen of the prairies—(I think we have seen at least a dozen of the species to-day)—is a scoundrel of much more imposing caliber. He delights to lurk around the outskirts of a herd of buffalo, keeping out of sight and unsuspected in the ravines and creek-timber, so far as possible; and wo to the unlucky calf that strays (which he seldom does) outside of the exterior line of defence formed by the bulls. If very large and hungry, the gray-wolf will sometimes manage to cut a cow off from the herd, and, interposing between her and her companions, detain or drive her further away, until she is beyond the hope of rescue, when her doom is sealed. His liveliest hope, however, is that of finding a buffalo whom some hunter has wounded, so that he cannot keep up with the herd, especially should it be stampeded. Let him once get such a one by himself, and a few snaps at his hamstrings, taking excellent care to keep out of the way of his horns, insures that the victim will have ceased to be a buffalo, and becomes mere wolf-meat before another morning."

Horace Greeley, *Overland Journey, from New York to San Francisco* (1860)

[156]

[122]

Grizzly Bear
LITHOGRAPH AFTER A DRAWING BY J. W. AUDUBON. 1848

"The Indians . . . consider the slaughter of a Grizzly Bear a feat second only to scalping an enemy, and necklaces made of the claws of this beast are worn as trophies by even the bravest among them. . . .

". . . During a voyage . . . up the Missouri river, a large she-Bear with two young was observed from the deck, and several gentlemen proposed to go ashore, kill the dam, and secure her cubs. A small boat was lowered . . . and with guns and ammunition they pushed off to the bank and landed in the mud.

"The old Bear had observed them and removed her position to some distance, where she stood near the bank . . . One of the hunters having neared the animal, fired at her, inflicting a severe wound. Enraged with pain the Bear rushed with open jaws towards the sportsmen . . . and with looks that assured them she was in a desperate fury. There was but a moment's time; the party, too much frightened to stand the charge, 'ingloriously turned and fled,' without even pulling another trigger, and darting to the margin of the river jumped into the stream, losing their guns, and floundering and bobbing under, while their hats floated away with the muddy current. After swimming a while they were picked up by the steamer, as terrified as if the Bear was even then among them, though the animal on seeing them all afloat had made off, followed by her young."

J. J. Audubon and John Bachman, *The Quadrupeds of North America* (1849)

[123]

The Lasso
BY WILLIAM T. RANNEY. 1846

"The tract of country over which we passed, between the False Washita and this place, is stocked, not only with buffaloes, but with numerous bands of wild horses, many of which we saw every day. There is no other animal on the prairies so wild and so sagacious as the horse; and none other so difficult to come up with. . . . In this herd we saw all the colours, nearly, that can be seen in a kennel of English hounds. Some were milk-white, some jet-black—others were sorrel, and bay, and cream colour—many were of an iron grey; and others were pied, containing a variety of colours on the same animal. Their manes were very profuse, and hanging in the wildest confusion over their necks and faces— and their long tails swept the ground. . . . The wild horse of these regions is a small, but very powerful animal; with an exceedingly prominent eye, sharp nose, high nostril, small feet and delicate leg; and undoubtedly, have sprung from a stock introduced by the Spaniards, at the time of the invasion of Mexico. . . . The usual mode of taking the wild horses, is, by throwing the lasso, whilst pursuing them at full speed, and dropping a noose over their necks, by which their speed is soon checked, and they are 'choked down'. The lasso is a thong of raw hide, some ten or fifteen yards in length, twisted or braided, with a noose fixed at the end of it; which, when the coil of the lasso is thrown out, drops with great certainty over the neck of the animal, which is soon conquered."

George Catlin, *North American Indians* (1841)

[158]

Buffaloes Crossing the Yellowstone
By CHARLES WIMAR. 1859

"The buffalo trails are always objects of interest and inquiry to the sight-seer on the Plains. These trails made by the herds in their migrating movements are so regular in their construction and course as to well excite curiosity. They vary but little from eight to ten inches in width, and are usually from two to four inches in depth; their course is almost as unvarying as that of the needle, running north and south. Of the thousands of buffalo trails which I have seen, I recollect none of which the general direction was not north and south. This may seem somewhat surprising at first thought, but it admits of a simple and satisfactory explanation.

"The general direction of all streams, large and small, on the Plains, is from the west to east, seeking as they do an entrance to the Mississippi. The habits of the buffalo incline him to graze and migrate from one stream to another, moving northward and crossing each in succession as he follows the young grass in the spring, and moving southward seeking the milder climate and open grazing in the fall and winter."

George A. Custer, *My Life on the Plains* (1874)

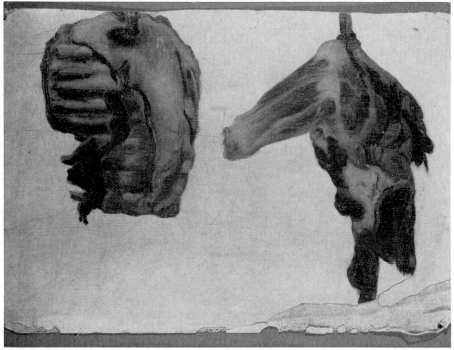

[125]

Studies of a Quartered Buffalo
By Charles Wimar. 1858

"Now, for the first time, he was initiated into the mysteries of 'butchering,' and watched the hunters as they turned the carcass on the belly, stretching out the legs to support it on each side. A transverse cut was then made at the nape of the neck, and gathering the long hair of the boss in one hand, the skin was separated from the shoulder. It was then laid open from this point to the tail, along the spine, and the skin was freed from the sides and pulled down to the brisket, but, still attached to it, was stretched upon the ground to receive the dissected portions. Then the shoulder was severed, the fleece removed from along the backbone, and the hump-ribs cut off with a tomahawk. All this was placed upon the skin; and after the 'boudins' had been withdrawn from the stomach, and the tongue—a great dainty—taken from the head, the meat was packed upon the mule, and the whole party hurried to camp rejoicing."

George Frederick Ruxton, *Life in the Far West* (1849)

[126]

Buffalo Bull

By ALBERT BIERSTADT. Probably 1858

"The favorite range of the buffalo is contained in a belt of country running north and south, about two hundred miles wide, and extending from the Platte River on the north to the valley of the Upper Canadian on the south. In migrating, if not grazing or alarmed, the buffalo invariably moves in single file, the column generally being headed by a patriarch of the herd, who is not only familiar with the topography of the country, but whose prowess in the field entitles him to become the leader of his herd. He maintains this leadership only so long as his strength and courage enable him to remain the successful champion in the innumerable contests which he is called upon to maintain."

George A. Custer, *My Life on the Plains* (1874)

Thunder Storm in the Rocky Mountains
BY ALBERT BIERSTADT. 1859

"While the deer are feeding, early in the morning and a short time before dark in the evening, are the best times to stalk them, as they are then busily occupied and less on the alert. When a deer is espied with his head down, cropping the grass, the hunter advances cautiously, keeping his eyes constantly directed upon him, and screening himself behind intervening objects, or, in the absence of other cover, crawls along upon his hands and knees in the grass, until the deer hears his steps and raises his head, when he must instantly stop and remain in an attitude fixed and motionless as a statue, for the animal's vision is his keenest sense. When alarmed he will detect the slightest movement of a small object, and, unless the hunter stands or lies perfectly still, his presence will be detected. If the hunter does not move, the deer will, after a short time, recover from his alarm, and resume his grazing, when he may be again approached. The deer always exhibits his alarm by a sudden jerking of the tail just before he raises his head."

Randolph B. Marcy, *The Prairie Traveler* (1863)

[128]

Wapiti

By William Jacob Hays. About 1865

"It is the same with the wapiti. Sometimes the park will be full of them; you may find herds feeding right down upon the plain among the cattle; and in a fortnight there will not be one left. All will have disappeared; and, what is more, it is almost impossible to follow them up and find them, for they are much shyer than the deer. Where do they go to? Not across the snowy range, certainly. Where, then? Up to the bare fells, just under the perpetual snow, where they crop the short sweet grass that springs amid the debris fallen from the highest peaks; to the deep, black recesses of primeval forest; to valleys, basins, little parks and plains, hidden among the folds of the mountains, where the foot even of the wandering miner has never disturbed the solitudes."

The Earl of Dunraven, *The Great Divide* (1876)

[129]

Cadaver of an Ox
By Frank Buchser. 1866

"Passed sixty or seventy dead oxen; it is supposed they have died from drinking at the poisoned springs. The men are naturally alarmed; but it appears more likely, judging from the poor condition they are in, that the long distances without water, and the scarcity of food, have been the causes of their death. The effluvium which proceeds from their carcasses is most disgusting, particularly when it is brought with a fair wind. Were they not so numerous the wolves would quickly remove them, but the supply being greater than the demand, beef is at such a discount that rot and the ravens have more matter than they can conveniently consume."

Henry J. Coke, *A Ride over the Rocky Mountains to Oregon and California* (1852)

The White Man

"THE ROMANCE OF THE WEST", a concept with which we are familiar from childhood, is in actuality a synthesis of the lives of the white men in their encounter with the great new world of the Louisiana Territory. The encounter is a matter of social history, of course, yet it is history so unexampled, so dramatic and so concerned with ordinary men struggling against huge odds or existing in circumstances so entirely different from their wont, that it has never ceased to capture the imagination and has taken on the hallowed tone of legend—of romance. Many artists of the nineteenth century saw this life as it unfolded, or read about it in the countless books and periodicals, in the journals, travels, reminiscences and adventures that poured from the presses of their day. They were alert to its significance, fascinated by its human interest, its drama and its poetry, just as their contemporaries were absorbed by the Indian, the wild life and the landscape of the West.

The Western pioneer, in search of new homes, of gold, of new opportunities and of religious freedom created history of such epic character that we could wish the pictorial record were more complete. But at least it is extremely varied and it covers a period of some eighty years. The following pages present a representative group of these pictures. Without reliance on portraits, they show us the men who habitually penetrated the farthest reaches of the frontier, the French Canadian voyageurs, the trappers and mountain men who traded with the Indians, the exemplar of the Western sportsman and adventurer, Captain William Drummond Stewart, the emigrants in their trains of covered wagons, the wayfarer in the wilderness, and the carefree boatmen of the wide rivers. They give us a glimpse of Army camp life on the Plains; they reveal the gentility of the inhabitants of the old French settlements; they emphasize the vigorous political life of the established communities of Missouri. As a companion of Bierstadt wrote from the Plains in 1858: "I doubt if there be any country but Kansas and Nebraska where the brush follows so hard on the rifle."

As in other aspects of the pictorial account of *Westward the Way* we rely upon artists of both renown and obscurity. Bingham and Bierstadt are bywords; but who has heard of Mrs. Abbe, of William Baldwin and Anna Maria von Phul? The latter young woman who migrated from Kentucky to St. Louis in the second decade of the nineteenth century created the only pictorial impression, except for portraits, of the inhabitants of the small Creole town near the confluence of the Mississippi and the Missouri about 1818. These little watercolors of exceptional charm and freshness vividly convey the refinement and grace that life assumed in a frontier community at an early date. Mrs. Abbe, about whom nothing seems to be known, painted at least one picture that is equally rare by virtue of its subject—*The Voyageur*. Only Charles Deas, who also recorded the trapper, and Caleb Bingham painted this extraordinary type of adventurer, guide and factotum who was indispensable in subduing the West, and only Mrs. Abbe attempted a close-up of his characteristic countenance.

Alfred Jacob Miller spent six months in the West, but with this short contact he contributed to it one of the most important chapters in its pictorial history. This young Baltimorean, trained in Paris, with a proficient watercolor technique at his fingertips, painted not only the extravagant aristocratic sportsman in his encounter with the West, but also the only pictures of a fur trader's caravan in action. For Captain William Drummond Stewart, Miller's patron, was making one of his numerous trips to the West and traveling on this occasion with the annual caravan of the Rocky Mountain Fur Company. The watercolors which were also important as the first pictures (after Seymour) of the Rocky Mountains and of all the wonderful landmarks that were soon to become familiar on the Oregon Trail, served Miller as models for many paintings of the West in later years.

Captain Seth Eastman, when stationed at Fort Snelling in Minnesota in the 'forties, and Charles Wimar, beginning with his boyhood in St. Louis, were primarily concerned in their artistic lives with the Plains Indian, but both men painted his inevitable clash with the white man in the thrilling subject of the emigrant train attacked by savages. Wimar worked out the subject in his Düsseldorf studio in two excellent compositions, the large cartoons for which are included here.

William Ranney, on the other hand, was interested only in the pioneer's adventures on the Great Plains. Born in Middletown, Connecticut and living most of his short life in New York and Hoboken, his brief experience on the Southwestern Plains as a recruit in the Mexican War, inspired him with the principal theme of his career—the pioneer and the trapper of the West; the danger, the fortitude, the tragedy and the exhilaration of their encounter with the frontier. Arthur Fitz William Tait, the English-born artist of New York, was similarly inspired although he never visited the West. His widespread reputation was made largely by the lithographic reproductions of his paintings by Currier and Ives.

At the same time in the 'forties and 'fifties, George Caleb Bingham of Missouri was creating his unexampled series of paintings of the boatmen's harum-scarum life on the rivers of the West and the lively political activity of Missouri, typical of the young towns that mushroomed as the frontier advanced. Occasionally a minor artist like the little known William Baldwin, who painted *The Merry Raftsmen*, or the bank note engravers of the day were attracted by these spheres of life; but actually Bingham's contribution to our knowledge of the white man in the West is unique. An active politician as well as an artist, he was unique in having grown up amidst the life he painted. His *Jolly Flatboatmen*, here published for the first time, made him famous and he justified his sudden reputation by repeated performances of similar merit. Amongst these are *The Wood-Boat, Captured by Indians* and *The Belated Wayfarers*, all three of which are also published here for the first time. His election series is not only remarkable artistically, but a precious document of the democratic process in America a century ago. Bingham's drawings of early Missouri types are as fine as any figure drawings produced in this country in the nineteenth century.

Albert Bierstadt, except in his beautiful oil sketches, saw the pioneer as he saw the Indian, as a detail of the frontier scene, his surpassing interest being the great mountains and the infinite skies of the West. Similarly, Frank Buchser, visiting the Plains in 1866, filled his sketch books with drawings of the settlers he encountered in the West; but they were of passing interest in his finished compositions.

The covered wagon, that undying symbol of the subjugation of the West, awaited the hand of Samuel Colman for its finest representation in the 'seventies. His *Emigrant Train Crossing Medicine Bow Creek* is a classic portrayal of that great subject, while his huge *Ships of the Plains* is probably the only painting of a freight caravan on the prairies, a sight which disappeared with the advent of the railroad.

The Indian fighters of the last two decades of the century, the cowboy and the rancher, were recorded by the painstaking Thomas Eakins, the Philadelphia realist, on a brief visit to the West in the 'eighties, while Frederic Remington celebrated their wild and exciting life on the Plains in a brilliant series of paintings familiar to almost everyone.

[130]

Keelboat on the Mississippi
LITHOGRAPH BY FELIX ACHILLE SAINT-AULAIRE. 1832

"Our barge was the best that ever ascended this river, and manned with twenty stout oars-men. Mr. Lisa, who had been a sea-captain, took much pains in rigging his boat with a good mast, and main and top-sail; these being great helps in the navigation of this river. Our equipage is chiefly composed of young men, though several have already made a voyage to the upper Missouri, of which they are exceedingly proud, and on that account claim a kind of precedence over the rest of the crew. We are in all, twenty-five men, and completely prepared for defence. There is, besides, a swivel on the bow of the boat, which, in case of attack, would make a formidable appearance; we have also two brass blunder-busses in the cabin, one over my birth, and the other over that of Mr. Lisa. These precautions were absolutely necessary from the hostility of the Sioux bands, who, of late had committed several murders and robberies on the whites, and manifested such a disposition that it was believed impossible for us to pass through their country. The greater part of the merchandise, which consisted of strouding, blankets, lead, tobacco, knifes, guns, beads, etc., was concealed in a false cabin, ingeniously contrived for the purpose; in this way presenting as little as possible to tempt the savages."

H. M. Brackenridge, *Journal of a Voyage Up the River Missouri in 1811* (1814)

Two Young Ladies [131]

Boy in Beaver Hat [1

Young Gentleman of Fashion [133]

St. Louis Belle [1

Young St. Louisans
By Anna Maria von Phul. About 1818

"The manners of the inhabitants are not different from those in other villages; we distinctly see the character of the ancient inhabitants, and of the new residents, and a compound of both. St. Louis, however, was always a place of more refinement and fashion, it is the residence of many genteel families, both French and American . . .

"In the character of these people, it must be remembered, that they are essentially Frenchmen; but, without that restlessness, impatience and fire, which distinguishes the European. There is, even in their deportment, something of the gravity of the Spaniard, though gay, and fond of amusements. . . . Instances of abandonment on the female side, or of seduction, are extremely rare. The women make faithful and affectionate wives, but will not be considered secondary in the matrimonial association. The advice of the wife is taken on all important, as well as on less weighty concerns, and she generally decides. . . .

"Their amusements were cards, billiards, and dances: this last of course the favourite. The dances were cotillions, reels, and sometimes the minuet. During the carnival, the balls follow in rapid succession. They have a variety of pleasing customs, connected with this amusement. Children have also their balls, and are taught a decorum and propriety of behavior, which is preserved through life. They have a certain ease and freedom of address, and are taught the secret of real politeness, *self denial*. . . . The American costume is generally introduced into the best families, and among the young girls and young men universally. I never saw any where greater elegance of dress than at the balls of St. Louis."

H. M. Brackenridge, *Views of Louisiana* (1814)

Merchant Taylor
Bernard Lalende
(Lately arrived from Bordeaux)

Takes the liberty to inform the public that he intends to follow the *Tayloring Business*, in all its branches, according to the latest fashions of Paris and London. He always takes this method of informing the Ladies and Gentlemen, that they will always be able to find at his shop, *Cloth* and other *Stuffs* of the best quality, suitable for dressing.

Also, that he has for sale various articles, such as *Embroidered patterns, Blue Handkerchiefs, White* and *Blue Thread, Bordeaux Wine, Coffee* and *Imperial Tea.—Also*, an assortment of the best *Fiddle-Strings*.

St. Louis, Sept. 6, 1809.

Missouri Gazette, Wednesday, October 4, 1809

Bull-boating

By Alfred Jacob Miller. 1837

"The water here being too deep to pass the goods in wagons, the bodies of the Conestoga wagons, or largest vehicles, have been dismounted; Buffalo hides secured over them and launched.

"The process of loading is commenced with certain mysterious boxes that have passed the frontiers without examination,—each of the boxes contain a keg holding about 10 gals. Alcohol,—on these are placed bales of goods consisting of blankets, cloths, calicoes, etc., then follow trunks and guns, and surmounting these are Indian women and children. The charettes (now empty) with their drivers are floated across and lastly the guards with a large band of reserve horses reach the banks—the latter refuse point blank to enter the water—the former are equally determined they shall,—so after indulging them in a little coquetry, no more time can be wasted,—the most turbulent and refractory are caught, carried to the edge of a bank, and pushed over;—the rebellion is at an end now, and the balance easily driven into the water."

Alfred Jacob Miller, *Notes* (1837) quoted in *The West of Alfred Jacob Miller*, edited by Marvin C. Ross, 1951

[136]

Prairie on Fire
By Alfred Jacob Miller. 1837

"Towards the Fall the grass, which has attained the height of 3 or 4 feet, becomes parched and dry.

"It is then very inflammable and either by accident or design takes fire. The manner of its approach is insidious enough; at first a slight haze is seen near the horizon, but the experienced eye of the Trapper or Indian immediately detects the nature of the visitor, and all hands in the camp are immediately busy in setting fire to the long grass about them;—not suffering it to make much headway, but beating it down with cloths and blankets. In this manner large spaces are cleared, horses, mules, and tents are secured in the burnt areas, which are enlarged as time permits, and escape from certain death is thus averted through a very simple process.

"The fire sweeps round with the speed of a race horse, licking up every thing that it touches with its fiery tongue,—leaving nothing in its train but a blackened heath."

Alfred Jacob Miller, *Notes* (1837) quoted in *The West of Alfred Jacob Miller*, edited by Marvin C. Ross, 1951

[137]

Rendezvous in the Wind River Mountains
BY ALFRED JACOB MILLER. About 1840

"At certain specified times during the year, the American Fur Company appoint a 'Rendezvous' at particular localities (selecting the most available spots) for the purpose of trading with Indians and Trappers, and here they congregate from all quarters. The first day is devoted to 'High Jinks,' a species of Saturnalia, in which feasting, drinking, and gambling form prominent parts.

"Sometimes an Indian becomes so excited with 'Fire Water' that he commences 'running a muck'—he is pursued, thrown or knocked down, and secured, in order to keep him from mischief. 'Affairs of honor' now and then are adjusted between rival Trappers—one of the parties, of course, receiving a complete drubbing;—all caused evidently from mixing too much Alcohol with their water. Night closes this scene of revelry and confusion. The following days exhibit the strongest contrast to this. The Fur Company's great tent is raised;— the Indians erect their picturesque white lodges;—The accumulated furs of the hunting season are brought forth, and the Company's tent is a besieged and busy place. Now the women come in for their share of ornaments and finery, being, as Tony Lumpkin expresses it, 'in a con-cat-enation accordingly.' The free trapper most especially bestowing presents on his favorite regardless of expense."

Alfred Jacob Miller, *Notes* (1837) quoted in *The West of Alfred Jacob Miller*, edited by Marvin C. Ross, 1951

Sir William Drummond Stewart's Caravan on the Platte
By ALFRED JACOB MILLER. About 1845

"The great scarcity of the Buffalo, through this country—a circumstance which afterwards was the cause of much suffering to the Emigrants—was attributable, in a great degree, to the presence of Sir William Stewart, with his pleasure party, and fifty or sixty fine horses for the chase; who, while we were passing through the Buffalo country, constantly kept several days ahead of us running, killing and driving the game out of reach. It was cheap sport to them, but dear to us; and we were led to conclude, that, if ever again an English or Scottish nobleman sees fit to look for pleasure in the Rocky Mountains, while an emigrating party is passing over them, it will be prudent to place him in the rear, instead of the van."

Overton Johnson and William H. Winter, *Route Across the Rocky Mountains* (1846)

"The section of country about the forks of the Platte is very pleasant, without any high mountains in sight; but at a distance beyond the widely extended rich bottom lands, bluffs of various forms present a picturesque scenery."

Samuel Parker, *Journal of an Exploring Tour* (1838)

[139]

The Voyageur
By Mrs. S. B. Abbe. About 1840

"Here are the descendants of the 'voyageurs,' the companions of LaSalle & Hennepin and they still retain their national distinctions. How different their manner, appearance & attitude from the 'Americans' around them. They have the vivacity, merry jest & laugh & expressive attitude and gesture of old france. They still speak french, which is heard as much as English and these two with Indian are often heard at once in the same group. They are generally of smaller size than the Americans & of light active figure, they are employed as boatmen, raftsmen and Indian traders. Most of them have Indian or half-breed wives which gives rise to another branch in the population of Minnesota. The scarf sash, pipe, & mocassins are the only remnants of the old voyageurs dress to be seen among them. The costume of the voyageurs was a mixture of Indian and European, a blanket coat reaching to about the knees, leggins and the breech-clout, & mocassins. The head was covered in summer with a fur or felt hat, adorned with feathers, the hat usually black & somewhat after the 'Spanish' form. Sometimes a close fitting woollen cap without visor—somewhat like a night-cap was worn."

Frank Blackwell Mayer, *With Pen and Pencil on the Frontier in 1851*, edited by Bertha L. Heilbron, 1932

[140]

The Trapper or Long Jakes

AFTER THE LOST ORIGINAL PAINTING BY CHARLES DEAS. About 1844

"These, nevertheless, were the men whose hardy enterprise opened to commerce and the plough the vast and fertile regions of the West. Rough and savage though they were, they alone were the pioneers of that extraordinary tide of civilisation which has poured its resistless current through tracts large enough for kings to govern; over a country now teeming with cultivation, where, a few short years ago, countless herds of buffalo roamed unmolested, the bear and deer abounded, and where the savage Indian skulked through the woods and prairies, lord of the unappreciated soil which now yields its prolific treasures to the spade and plough of civilised man. To the wild and half-savage trapper, who may be said to exhibit the energy, enterprise, and hardihood charactertistic of the American people, divested of all the false and vicious glare with which a high state of civilization, too rapidly attained, has obscured their real and genuine character, in which the above traits are eminently prominent—to these men alone is due the empire of the West—destined in a few short years to become the most important of those confederate states which compose the mighty union of North America."

George Frederick Ruxton, *Life in the Far West* (1849)

[177]

[141]

Emigrants Attacked by the Comanches
By Seth Eastman. About 1845

"When a halt is made the wagons are 'corraled,' as it is called, by bringing the two front ones near and parallel to each other. The two next are then driven up on the outside of these, with the front wheels of the former touching the rear wheels of the latter, the rear of the wagons turned out upon the circumference of the circle that is being formed, and so on, until one-half the circle is made, when the rear of the wagons are turned in to complete the circle. An opening of about twenty yards should be left between the last two wagons for animals to pass in and out of the corral, and this may be closed with two ropes stretched between the wagons. Such a corral forms an excellent and secure barricade against Indian attacks, and a good inclosure for cattle while they are being yoked: indeed, it is indispensable."

Randolph B. Marcy, *The Prairie Traveler* (1863)

[142]

The Prairie Fire
By William T. Ranney. 1848

"The polar-star by its 'pointers' had just told the hour of midnight, when these hurried words rang through the camp:

" 'Lave, ho! Lave! Prairies on fire! Quick—catch up! catch up!'

"This startling announcement instantly brought every man to his feet;—and such a scene as now met the eye! How awful, and how grand! The wind, new changed and freshened, to the right and rear, was tossing the flames towards us, rapidly —lighting the heavens with their lurid glare, and transforming the darkness of night into a more than noon-day splendor!

. . . "We were speedily under way, with as much earnestness of advance as that of righteous Lot, in his escape from burning Sodom. For a while the pursuing enemy kept even pace, and threatened to overtake us, till, headed by the strong wind, which meanwhile had changed its course, it began to slacken its speed and abate its greediness."

Rufus B. Sage, *Scenes in the Rocky Mountains* (1846)

[143]

Prairie Burial
By William T. Ranney. 1848

"These were the first emigrants we had overtaken, although we had found abundant and melancholy traces of their progress throughout the course of the journey. Sometimes we passed the grave of one who had sickened and died on the way. The earth was usually torn up and covered by wolf tracks. Some had escaped this violation. One morning a piece of plank, standing upright on the summit of a grassy hill attracted our notice, and riding up to it, we found the following words, very roughly traced upon it, apparently with a red hot piece of iron:

Mary Ellis
Died May 7th, 1845
Aged two months

Francis Parkman, *The California and Oregon Trail* (1849)

The Pioneers

By William T. Ranney. About 1850

"When the march is to extend 1500 or 2000 miles, or over a rough sandy or muddy road, I believe young oxen will endure better than mules; they will, if properly managed, keep in better condition, and perform the journey in an equally brief space of time. . . . Ox-traveling, when once a man becomes accustomed to it, is not so disagreeable as might be expected, particularly if one succeeds in obtaining a tractable animal. On emergencies, an ox can be made to proceed at a tolerably quick pace; for, though his walk is only about three miles an hour at an average, he may be made to perform double that distance in the same time. Mr. Galton once accomplished twenty-four miles in four hours, and that, too, through heavy sand!"

Randolph B. Marcy, *The Prairie Traveler* (1863)

Caravan on the Prairies
BY WILLIAM T. RANNEY. About 1850

"Wagons should be of the simplest possible construction—strong, light, and made of well-seasoned timber, especially the wheels, as the atmosphere, in the elevated and arid region over which they have to pass, is so exceedingly dry during the summer months, that unless the wood-work is thoroughly seasoned, they will require constant repairs to prevent them from falling to pieces.

"Wheels made of the bois-d'arc, or Osage orange-wood, are the best for the plains, as they shrink but little, and seldom want repairing. As, however, this wood is not easily procured in the Northern States, white oak answers a very good purpose if well seasoned."

Randolph B. Marcy, *The Prairie Traveler* (1863)

[146]

The Trappers
By William T. Ranney. About 1850

"Prior to the time of which we write, adventurous hunters and trappers had plied their vocation along the line of the Missouri River to its source in the mountains, there striking the head waters of the Columbia and following that stream to the trading posts of the American Fur Company on the Pacific Coast, where they squandered the proceeds from the sale of their peltries in riotous living, returning the next season over the same route to St. Louis, where they spent the winter as hale fellows well met. They traveled in parties of three or more, in order to better protect themselves from hostile Indians. Their rifles furnished them with food and they slept under the stars without shelter, enjoying perfect health in the pure mountain air, and were never so happy as when fraternizing with, or fighting, Indians."

Reuben Cole Shaw, *Across the Plains in Forty-nine* (1896)

The Retreat
By WILLIAM T. RANNEY. 1850

"A small number of white men, in traveling upon the Plains, should not allow a party of strange Indians to approach them unless able to resist an attack under the most unfavorable circumstances.

"It is a safe rule, when a man finds himself alone in the prairies, and sees a party of Indians approaching, not to allow them to come near him, and if they persist in so doing, to signal them to keep away. If they do not obey, and he be mounted upon a fleet horse, he should make for the nearest timber. If the Indians follow and press him too closely, he should halt, turn around, and point his gun at the foremost, which will often have the effect of turning them back, but he should never draw trigger unless he finds that his life depends upon the shot; for, as soon as his gun is discharged, his sole dependence, unless he have time to reload, must be upon the speed of his horse."

Randolph B. Marcy, *Thirty Years of Army Life on the Border* (1866)

The Scouting Party
By WILLIAM T. RANNEY. About 1851

"What distance are you west of Yellow Stone here, my good fellow?
Comment?
What distance?—(stop)—quel distance?
Pardón, Monsieur, Je ne sais pas, Monsieur.
Ne Parlez vous l'Anglais?
Non, Monsr. I speaks de French and de Americaine; mais je ne parle pas l'Anglais.
Well, then, my good fellow, I will speak English, and you may speak Americaine.
Pardón, pardón, Monsieur.
Well, then, we will both speak Americaine.
Val, sare, je suis bien content, pour for I see dat you speaks putty coot Americaine."

George Catlin, *North American Indians* (1841)

Many of the seasoned and most expert mountain men and trappers were French Canadians who were more apt to be proficient in the Indian tongues than in English.

[149]

The Merry Raftsmen
By William Baldwin. 1844

"No wonder, that to the young, who are reared in these remote regions, with that restless curiosity, which is fostered by solitude and silence, and who witness scenes like this so frequently, the severe and unremitting labors of agriculture, performed directly in the view of such spectacles, would become tasteless and irksome. No wonder, that the young, along the banks of the great streams, should detest the labors of the field, and embrace every opportunity, either openly, or, if minors, covertly to escape, and devote themselves to the pernicious employment of boating."

Timothy Flint, *The History and Geography of the Mississippi Valley* (1831)

[150]

The Jolly Flatboatmen
By George Caleb Bingham. 1844

"Nor is there any wonder that the mode of life pursued by these boatmen should have presented irresistible seductions to the young people along the banks. Fancy one of these huge boats dropping lazily along with the current past their cabins on a balmy morning in June. Picture to your imagination the gorgeous foliage; the soft, delicious temperature of the atmosphere; the deep azure of the sky; the fertile alluvion, with its stupendous forests and rivers; the romantic bluffs sleeping mistily in blue distance; the clear waters rolling calmly adown, with the woodlands outlined in shadow on the surface; the boat floating leisurely onward, its heterogeneous crew of all ages dancing to the violin upon the deck, flinging out their merry salutations among the settlers, who come down to the water's edge to see the pageant pass, until, at length, it disappears behind a point of wood, and the boatman's bugle strikes up its note, dying in distance over the waters."

Edmund Flagg, *The Far West* (1838)

This classic of American genre painting, Bingham's most famous canvas which earned him the title of "The Missouri Artist", is here published for the first time. Long thought to have been lost, it was reproduced as a steel engraving by the American Art Union in 1847 and widely distributed.

Negro Boy [151]

Bull-Whacker [152]

Respected Citizen [153]

[154]

Man Listening to a Speech

Farm Hand   [155]   *Wayfarer*   [156]

Men of Missouri

BY GEORGE CALEB BINGHAM. About 1850

"In St. Louis, society exhibits the same aspect as in other towns of a like size in the United States. The roughness of the backwoodsman is often, however, accompanied with an open hospitality, an honest simplicity, a genuine kindness of heart, which render a residence among them quite as pleasant as in those regions where observance and public opinion have created a greater degree of apparent refinement. It might be expected, that a country almost boundless, with few barriers of law, or local limits of habitancy and property, an extent of nearly one thousand leagues towards the western sea, would be the natural resort of wild and adventurous spirits, whose object was, as they often express it, to fly 'beyond Sabbath.' It is so in fact. But there is more order and quietness, regulated society, and correct public opinion, than in such a state of things we should have a right to expect."

Timothy Flint, *The History and Geography of the Mississippi Valley* (1831)

[189]

[157]

Shooting for the Beef
By George Caleb Bingham. 1850

"As I rode along through the country I was somewhat surprised at meeting people from various quarters, who seemed to be gathering to some rendezvous, all armed with rifles, and with the paraphernalia of hunting suspended from their shoulders. At length, near noon, I passed a log-cabin, around which were assembled about a hundred men; and, upon inquiry, I learned that they had come together for the purpose of 'shooting a beeve' (or beef), as the marksmen have it. The regulations I found to be chiefly these: A bull's-eye, with a centre nail, stands at a distance variously of from forty to seventy yards; and those five who, at the close of the contest, have most frequently *driven the nail*, are entitled to a fat ox divided into five portions. Many of the marksmen in the vicinity, I was informed, could drive the nail twice out of every three trials."

Edmund Flagg, *The Far West* (1838)

[158]

The Wood-Boat

By George Caleb Bingham. 1850

"As the Steam-boats on the Mississippi, and indeed all over America, burn nothing but wood, it becomes necessary to make occasional stops to replenish their stock of fuel. Accordingly, on the banks of the great rivers—which are all now covered with these vessels—many settlers find it a profitable occupation to devote themselves exclusively to preparing stacks of firewood, close to the bank, ready for the boats as they pass, either by day or by night . . .

". . . The price per cord varies from a dollar and a half, to three dollars. A cord consists of a heap or stack, eight feet long by four high, each billet in the pile being four feet in length."

Basil Hall, *Forty Etchings, from Sketches made with the Camera Lucida, in North America* (1829)

[159]

The County Election
BY GEORGE CALEB BINGHAM. 1851

"A rougher set of citizens, whether regarded with reference to dress, manners or physical appearance, separately or combined, could not be imagined. . . . Tall, square-shouldered, broad-chested, stout men, made up of bone and gristle, they drank whiskey, chewed tobacco, and while waiting for the opening of Court, engaged in athletic sports in front of the temple of Thetis. . . . Their general good humour, and the excellent temper with which they bore their reverses was admirable, until towards evening, when fiery liquor caused many to lose their heads."

John Lewis Peyton, *Over the Alleghanies and Across the Prairies* (1869)

[160]

Stump Speaking
By George Caleb Bingham. 1854

"Here we saw . . . crowds of politicians indulging in a last harangue upon the topics of the day. Prairie farmers, pig-drivers, huntsmen, Indians, half-breeds, and labourers were assembled to hear the stump orator's last appeal, and to indulge in a preliminary glass previous to the 'big drunk,' as the Indians call it, with which so large a part of the population out West close the important event of the Presidential election."

John Lewis Peyton, *Over the Alleghanies and Across the Prairies* (1869)

[161]

The Verdict of the People
BY GEORGE CALEB BINGHAM. 1854-55

"I have already commenced thinking for another large composition, which I will entitle *The Verdict of the People*. I intend it to be a representation of the scene that takes place at the close of an exciting political contest, just when the final result of the ballot is proclaimed from the stand of [the] judges. The subject will doubtless strike you as one well calculated to furnish that contrast and variety of expression which confers the chief value upon pictures of this class. I might very properly introduce into it some of those comically long faces which were seen about Fayette, Missouri when our friend Claib (Claiborne F. Jackson) was so genteelly whipped last summer. . . . It is much larger and will contain more striking points than either of its predecessors [*Stump Speaking and County Election*]. I desire it to cap the climax."

George Caleb Bingham, *Letter* dated Philadelphia, April 10, 1854 quoted by C. B. Rollins in *Some Recollections of George Caleb Bingham* (1926)

[162]

Captured by Indians

By George Caleb Bingham. Probably 1856

"The Indian has become the foe of peace, the foe of humanity, the foe of civilization. He might have abided with and acquired all with profit, and preserved his race indefinitely; but every effort to better his condition has been responded to with savage treachery and with defiance of all the instincts of chivalry and mercy. His chief ambition is not merely to murder alike innocent and guilty, friend and foe, but he is master of the most exquisite tortures to practice upon his victims. He dooms his female captives to wrongs so cruel that language is beggared to portray them; and his proudest trophies are the silken tresses of the wives and daughters of the pale-faces."

A. K. McClure, *Three Thousand Miles through the Rocky Mountains* (1869)

[163]

The Belated Wayfarers
By George Caleb Bingham. About 1856

" 'Well,' said the sergeant, a thorough-bred woodsman, 'star or no star, I have passed many a night alone in a wilder place than this, and slept sound, too, I'll warrant you. Once, however, I had rather an uneasy time of it. I was belated in passing through a tract of wood; . . . so I struck a light, made a fire, and turned my horse loose, while I stretched myself to sleep. By and by, I heard the wolves howl. My horse came crowding near me for protection, for he was terribly frightened. After a while, I heard a strange dismal cry. I thought at first it might be an owl. I heard it again, and then I knew it was not an owl, but must be a panther. I felt rather awkward, for I had no weapon but a double-bladed penknife. I however prepared for defence in the best way I could, and piled up small brands from the fire, to pepper him with, should he come nigh. The company of my horse now seemed a comfort to me. . . . I kept watch, and nodded and dozed, and started awake, and looked round, expecting to see the glaring eyes of the panther close upon me; but somehow or other, fatigue got the better of me, and I fell asleep outright. In the morning I found the tracks of a panther within sixty paces. They were as large as my two fists. He had evidently been walking backwards and forwards, trying to make up his mind to attack me; but luckily, he had not courage.' "

Washington Irving, *A Tour on the Prairies* (1835)

[196]

[164]

Attack on an Emigrant Train
By Charles Wimar. 1854

"I beg to impress this important and, to Western men, self-evident truth upon your readers and the national authorities,—that there are no friendly Indians on the Plains. There has been no peace since the settlement of Colorado, although hostile tribes have not confederated to make war until recently. There is not a single nomadic tribe east of the mountains that is at heart friendly with the whites,—not one that does not, when opportunity is offered with apparent safety, steal, and murder if necessary, and often murder wantonly.

"The Indian, in his nomadic state, must henceforth be at war with the white man; and one or the other must recede. The time was when he could be at peace, when his hunting grounds were not encroached upon by the march of civilization, and he met his rivals only on his borders to traffic with them. Now the surges of progress break upon his buffalo and deer from both the Atlantic and the Pacific."

A. K. McClure, *Three Thousand Miles through the Rocky Mountains* (1869)

Attack on an Emigrant Train
By CHARLES WIMAR. 1856

". . . Imagine our consternation and dismay, when, upon descending into the valley of the Cimarron, on the morning of the 19th of June, a band of Indian warriors on horseback suddenly appeared before us from behind the ravines— an imposing array of death-dealing savages! There was no merriment in this! It was a genuine alarm—a tangible reality! These warriors, however, as we soon discovered, were only the van-guard of a 'countless host,' who were by this time pouring over the opposite ridge, and galloping directly towards us.

"The wagons were soon irregularly 'formed' upon the hillside: but in accordance with the habitual carelessness of caravan traders, a great portion of the men were unprepared for the emergency. Scores of guns were 'empty,' and as many more had been wetted by the recent showers, and would not 'go off.' Here was one calling for balls—another for powder—a third for flints. Exclamations, such as, 'I've split my caps'—'I've rammed down a ball without powder'— 'My gun is choked, give me yours'—were heard from different quarters; while a timorous 'greenhorn' would perhaps cry out, 'Here, take my gun, you can outshoot me!' . . . The Indians who were in advance made a bold attempt to press upon us, which came near costing them dearly; for some of our fiery backwoodsmen more than once had their rusty but unerring rifles directed upon the intruders, . . . The savages made demonstrations no less hostile, rushing, with ready sprung bows, upon a portion of our men who had gone in search of water."

Josiah Gregg, *Commerce of the Prairies* (1844)

[166]

Turf House on the Plains
By Charles Wimar. About 1860

"The region is substantially uninhabitable; every ten or fifteen miles is a stable
of the stage proprietor, and every other ten or fifteen miles an eating-house;
perhaps as often a petty ranch or farmhouse, whose owner lives by selling hay to
the trains of emigrants or freighter; every fifty to one hundred miles you will find
a small grocery and blacksmith shop; and about as frequently is a military station
with a company or two of United States troops for protection againts the Indians.
This makes up all the civilization of the Plains. The barns and houses are of
logs or prairie turf, piled up layer on layer, and smeared over or between with
a clayey mud. The turf and mud make the best houses, and the same material
is used for military forts and for fences around the cattle and horse yards. Their
roofs, where covered, are a foot thickness of turfs, sand, clay, and logs or twigs,
with an occasional inside lining of skins or thick cloth."

Samuel Bowles, *Across the Continent* (1865)

[167]

American Frontier Life
BY ARTHUR FITZ WILLIAM TAIT. 1852

"The American trapper stands by himself, and is peerless for the service of the wilderness. Drop him in the midst of a prairie, or in the heart of the mountains, and he is never at a loss. He notices every landmark; can retrace his route through the most monotonous plains, or the most perplexed labyrinths of the mountains; no danger nor difficulty can appal him, and he scorns to complain under any privation. In equipping the two kinds of trappers, the creole and Canadian are apt to prefer the light fusee; the American always grasps the rifle: he despises what he calls the 'shot-gun'. We give these estimates on the authority of a trader of long experience, and a foreigner by birth. 'I consider one American,' said he, 'equal to three Canadians in point of sagacity, aptness at resources, self-dependence, and fearlessness of spirit. In fact, no one can cope with him as a stark tramper of the wilderness.'"

Washington Irving, *The Rocky Mountains* (1837)

The Rocky Mountains—Emigrants Crossing the Plains   [168]
Lithograph after a drawing by Frances F. Palmer. 1866

"And the Rocky Mountains, with the grand, aromatic forests, their grassy glades, their frequent springs, and dancing streams of the brightest, sweetest water, their pure, elastic atmosphere, and their unequalled game and fish, are destined to be a favorite resort and home of civilized man. I never visited a region where physical life could be more surely prolonged or fully enjoyed. Thousands who rush hither for gold will rush away again disappointed and disgusted, as thousands have already done; and yet the gold is in these mountains, and the right man will gradually unearth it."

Horace Greeley, *An Overland Journey, from New York to San Francisco* (1860)

[169]

Trappers at Fault Looking for the Trail
By Arthur Fitz William Tait. About 1860

"In trailing horses, there will be no trouble while the ground is soft, as the impressions they leave will then be deep and distinct; but when they pass over hard or rocky ground, it is sometimes a very slow and troublesome process to follow them. Where there is grass, the trace can be seen for a considerable time, as the grass will be trodden down and bent in the direction the party has moved; should the grass have returned to its upright position, the trail can often be distinguished by standing upon it and looking ahead for some distance in the direction it has been pursuing; the grass that has been turned over will show a different shade of green from that around it, and this often marks a trail for a long time."

Randolph B. Marcy, *The Prairie Traveler* (1863)

[170]

Nooning on the Platte
By ALBERT BIERSTADT. Probably 1858

"In traveling with ox teams in the summer season, great benefit will be derived from making early marches; starting with the dawn, and making a 'nooning' during the heat of the day, as oxen suffer much from the heat of the sun in the midsummer. These noon halts should, if possible, be so arranged as to be near grass and water, where the animals can improve their time in grazing. When it gets cool, they may be hitched to the wagons again, and the journey continued in the afternoon. Sixteen or eighteen miles a day may thus be made without injury to the beast, and longer drives can never be expedient, unless in order to reach grass or water. When the requisites for encamping cannot be found at the desired intervals, it is better for the animals to make a very long drive than to encamp without water or grass. The noon halt in such cases may be made without water, and the evening drive lengthened."

Randolph B. Marcy, *The Prairie Traveler* (1863)

[171]

Surveyor's Wagon in the Rockies
By ALBERT BIERSTADT. Probably 1858

"In the midst of these scenes of exuberant and solitary Nature, what a school for the artist alive to her glories, and patiently receptive of her teachings! After a day's travel in a spring-wagon, Bierstadt, his companion, and their servant would start on Indian ponies and ramble for miles, to explore, to kill game for their supper, and to sketch. Grouse, antelope, rabbits, wild ducks and sage hens, with coffee and corn-bread, furnished their repast; they slept in blankets under the open sky, and woke up with dew on their faces. This life invigorated body and mind, exhilarated the spirits, and freshened that love of and intimacy with nature, whence the true artist draws his best inspiration. It was thus that the landscape of the Rocky Mountains was studied; the trees, peaks, fertile levels, barren ridges, atmospheric effects, Indian costumes, accoutrements, physiognomies—each element and aspect of the country was delineated with conscientious skill, and from these was executed a grand historical and geographical picture of the Wind River range in Nebraska Territory. To one who has never visited the scene, perhaps the best proof of the authentic merits of the landscape may be derived from the vivid description of an enthusiastic lover of nature, who, long before this picture was achieved, attempted to convey his impressions of this scenery in words which partook equally of artistic and poetical enthusiasm."

Henry T. Tuckerman, *Book of the Artists* (1867)

[203]

[172]

The Oregon Trail
BY ALBERT BIERSTADT. About 1865

"We are now upon the main road over which all emigrants must pass, whether bound for Oregon or California. It is nearly a continuous, unbroken procession. We pass the ferrying-place, leaving it three miles to the left. We learn that seven thousand teams have already crossed this ferry the present season. Thousands have crossed at various points below, and other thousands are now passing who do not cross the river at all."

Franklin Langworthy, *Scenery of the Plains, Mountains and Mines* (1855)

"This is the great emigrant route from Missouri to California and Oregon, over which so many thousands have traveled within the past few years. The track is broad, well worn, and cannot be mistaken. It has received the major part of the Mormon emigration, and was traversed by the army in its march to Utah in 1857 . . . Many persons who have had much experience in prairie-traveling prefer leaving the Missouri River in March or April, and giving grain to their animals until the new grass appears. The roads become muddy and heavy after the spring rains set in, and by starting out early the worst part of the road will be passed over before the ground becomes wet and soft . . . As large numbers of cattle pass over the road annually, they soon consume all the grass in these barren localities, and such as pass late in the season are likely to suffer greatly, and oftentimes perish from starvation. When I came over the road in August, 1858, I seldom found myself out of sight of dead cattle for 500 miles along the road."

Randolph B. Marcy, *The Prairie Traveler* (1863)

[173]

Ford on the Platte
By Frank Buchser. 1866

"In a large company of men, horses, wagons, and equipments, the crossing of rivers is quite an undertaking and, if deep, involving considerable risk and damage. . . . In the first place guides are sent out to cross and explore the river at different points, in order to find the best places for embarking and landing, and when the river is deep, the goods must be all unladen from about 30 wagons and charettes, transferred to boats, and ferried across.

"The horses and mules compelled to swim, and *nolens volens* pitched into the river to take their chances, there is a great deal of fun and merriment intermingled with hard swearing in several languages.—The trappers getting rid of their religion and losing their temper at the same time. Sterne's Capt. Shandy remarked that 'our army swore terribly in Flanders.' In this particular accomplishment, our devil-may-care Trappers have not degenerated."

Alfred Jacob Miller, *Notes* (1837) quoted in *The West of Alfred Jacob Miller*, edited by Marvin C. Ross, 1951

Tent Encampment at Night
By Frank Buchser. 1866

"On the right of our tent [in General Custer's Camp, 1868] began the others
—one for guests, another for the dining-tent, then the round Sibley, that General
Custer had used during the winter, for the cook tent. This must have been
modelled after an Indian tepee, as it looked much like it. At that time Sibley
tents were not in use, but why, we could never understand, as the wind had
so little purchase upon them, finding no corners to toy with, that this circular
house could almost defy a hurricane. The fire was built in the centre, and
the smoke escaped through an aperture at the top, which could be half covered,
according to the direction of the wind, by pulling ropes attached to a little
fly. The Indians had the same arrangement, only they managed the opening
a little better."

Elizabeth B. Custer, *Following the Guidon* (1890)

"The nights . . . were peculiarly beautiful when cloudless. The rarity of the
atmosphere gave full play to the star-beams, and it seemed as if there were
twice as many as in any firmament elsewhere.
"Their first appearance was often mistaken for Indian signal fires, as they rose
above the horizon, like the sun or moon, having orbs as marked and light as
brilliant as when they attained the zenith."

Margaret I. Carrington, *Absaraka Home of the Crows* (1868)

[175]

Sunrise: Laramie Plains
BY FRANK BUCHSER. 1866

"Daylight was beginning to make its appearance in the east when our little party of slumbering troopers began to arouse themselves. Those unfortunate persons who have always been accustomed to the easy comforts of civilization, and who have never known what real fatigue or hunger is, cannot realize or appreciate the blissful luxury of a sleep which follows a day's ride in the saddle of half a hundred miles or more.

"Being the first to awake, I rose to a sitting posture and took a hasty survey of our situation. Within a few feet of us flowed the Platte River. Our group, horses and men, presented an interesting subject for a painter. To my surprise I discovered that a heavy shower of rain had fallen during the night, but so deep had been our slumber that even the rain had failed to disturb us. Each one of the party had spread his saddle blanket on the ground to serve as his couch, while for covering we had called into requisition the india-rubber poncho or rubber blanket which invariably forms an important part of the Plainsman's outfit. The rain, without awakening any of the party, had aroused them sufficiently to cause each one to pull his rubber blanket over his face and thus protected he continued his repose. The appearance presented by this somber-looking group of sleepers strongly reminded me of scenes during the war when, after a battle, the bodies of the slain had been collected for burial."

George A. Custer, *My Life on the Plains* (1874)

Consultation   [176]
BY FRANK BUCHSER. 1866

"Virginia Dale deserves its pretty name. A pearly, lively-looking stream runs
through a beautiful basin, of perhaps one hundred acres, among the mountains,
—for we are within the embrace of the great hills,—stretching away in smooth
and rising pasture to nooks and crannies of the wooded range; fronted by rock
embattlement, and flanked by the snowy peaks themselves; warm with a June
sun, and rare and pure with an air into which no fetid breath has poured itself,
—it is difficult to imagine a more lovable spot in nature's kingdom."

Samuel Bowles, *Across the Continent* (1865)

The Last Moment in Virginia Dale   [177]
BY FRANK BUCHSER. 1866

"Under the most auspicious circumstances, and in time of peace with the Indians,
the life of an army officer on the Plains or along our frontier is at best one
involving no little personal discomfort, and demanding the sacrifice of many of
the luxuries and benefits which he could obtain were he located within the limits
of civilization. To many officers, service in the West amounts almost to social
exile. Some can have their families with or near them. There is a limited
opportunity for social intercourse; travel from the States, to and across the
Plains, either for business or pleasure, is uninterrupted, and mail facilities with
friends and relations in the States are maintained."

George A. Custer, *My Life on the Plains* (1874)

Return from Idaho to Virginia Dale   .   [178]
BY FRANK BUCHSER. 1866

"The day's ride ended at Virginia Dale, where we got a tolerable dinner, and
found an exquisite little valley, as if nature was trying just there quite to outdo
herself. Abrupt mountains tower all around and shut it in like a picture, while
the entrance to and exit from the vale are bold and precipitous. With its limpid
stream, green sward, and bristling pines, it seemed like an oasis in the desert of
the foot-hills there; and a party of miners encamped there for the night, en route
from Montana to the States, appeared to enjoy its freshness and beauty to the
full."

James R. Rusling, *Across America* (1874)

Covered Wagons Crossing Medicine Bow Creek
By Samuel Colman. 1870

"We crossed the river at the first ford, and entered the rocky gorge through which the river flowed, and proceeded about a mile to the second ford. A narrow pathway had been cut in the bank, capable of admitting but one wagon at a time, and the ford was so deep that every wagon had to be raised about six inches from its bed to prevent water from flowing in. The ford was crooked and bad, and a large number of teams were in advance of us, which would detain us till noon before our turn would come to cross."

Alonzo Delano, *Across the Plains and Among the Diggings* (1853)

"Drove 17 miles road sandy the country around looks so desolate no timbe[r] to be seen and scarcely any grass the road crosses a number of ravines sand from 8 to 10 inches deep and very hard pulling for the oxen we passed castel bluffs this forenoon they raise to the hight of three hundred feet from the surface of the plains they are covered withed small stunted cedars we have had several showers of rain during the day it rained all last night but had no wind with it which is something remarkable camp half a mile from the river water & grass good."

Joseph Hackney, *Diary* (1849) quoted in *Wagons West* by Elizabeth Page, 1930

[180]

Ships of the Plains
BY SAMUEL COLMAN. 1872

" . . . the long trains of wagons and carts, with their teams of mules and oxen, passing to and fro on the road, going in empty, coming out laden with corn for man and beast, with machinery for the mining regions, with clothing, food and luxuries for the accumulating populations of Colorado, Utah and Montana, for all these territories and the intermediate populations draw their supplies from this quarter, and not from the California shore. The wagons are covered with white cloth; each is drawn by four to six pairs of mules or oxen; and the trains of them stretch frequently from one-quarter to one-third of a mile each. As they move along in the distance, they remind one of the caravans described in the Bible and other Eastern books."

Samuel Bowles, *Across the Continent* (1865)

This is one of the rare representations of an overland cargo wagon train in the West. The emigrant trains were a favorite subject.

Cowboys in the Bad Lands
BY THOMAS EAKINS. 1888

"A few pines and junipers appear here and there, and on the declivities small patches of grass, like Alpine meadows, so that we could fancy ourselves now in Switzerland, now in the valley of the Rhine; but the naked rude character of the Mauvaises Terres seems to be unique in its kind, and this impression is strengthened when you look up and down the river. Only the croaking of the raven was heard in this desolate waste, which even the Indian avoids, and very unwillingly visits these steep mountains. As those people generally travel on horseback, they prefer the open prairies beyond the mountains, where they usually find the herds of buffaloes."

Maximilian, Prince of Wied, *Travels in the Interior of North America* (1843)

The Settlements: Forts, Towns and Cities

IN 1804 WHEN the United States doubled its size by the purchase of Louisiana, there were in that nearly one million square miles of wilderness two important settlements, New Orleans and St. Louis. The others were scattered hamlets or fur traders' posts also situated on the great river which afforded their only means of communication. The transfer of the huge domain offered a new inducement to the westward migration of Americans and a steady and ever increasing stream of settlers began to cross the Mississippi. The old settlements grew and new ones sprang up. A thousand miles beyond the Father of Waters the fortified posts of the fur traders multiplied and in time were supplemented by the frontier forts of the Army as a protection against the Indians. A spirit of pride in this prodigious and swift accomplishment was soon reflected in the portraits of the new habitations of the white man. With some artists, stimulated by the avid interest of armchair travellers, it became a field of specialized endeavor.

The pride that motivated this activity was apparent in the first of such views that the obscure topographic artist, Bouquet de Woiseri, made of New Orleans in 1804. Above the town he painted an American eagle clutching a starry banner on which was proclaimed, "Under my wings everything prospers." This spirit of pride, patriotism and optimism continued to inspire his numerous successors, the most important of whom was John Casper Wild, the Swiss who specialized in the field, having come first to Philadelphia, then settled in St. Louis about 1840, and died in Davenport, Iowa in 1846. His few years on the Mississippi produced a series of paintings that were reproduced in thirty-four lithographs in his *Valley of the Mississippi Illustrated.* Similarly, the English-born Henry Lewis who settled in St. Louis about 1836 is best known for his lavishly illustrated volume called *Das Illustrirte Mississippithal*, published in Germany from 1854-1858 and containing seventy-eight lithographs after his drawings of the towns and landscape of the great river. In Nebraska and Montana and chiefly in Colorado,

Alfred E. Mathews, who was also born in England, distinguished himself as a consistent portrayer of the raw young towns of the West in the 'sixties, having attracted attention for the skill he displayed in draftsmanship as a soldier in the Union Army. Like his predecessors he saw to it that his works were published in book form and, like the earlier works, the four volumes containing his drawings as lithographs —*Pencil Sketches of Colorado, Pencil Sketches of Montana, Scenes of Rocky Mountain Scenery* and *Canyon City, Colorado, and Its Surroundings*—have become choice collector's items.

There were also many obscure artists who turned their eyes to what the white man had created in the wilderness, as well as three more famous who left their record of the settlements as an adjunct of their larger concern. Of the former there is Anna Maria von Phul who in her watercolor art painted the very early views of St. Louis, her new home, about 1818; and the soldier Hermann Stieffel who painted the rare views of the Army forts of the West where his company was stationed in the 'seventies, and the more accomplished Vincent Colyer whose interest was of a similar kind. Many other obscure artists and commercial draftsmen of the second half of the century were employed by publishing houses to prepare the panoramic views for lithographic prints of the young towns and cities, not excluding the jerry-built boom towns of the miners in the mountain pockets of Colorado, that were beginning to feel their importance. Of these a small but representative group is included in the following pages.

The great painters of the Indians have also left precious records of the settlements. Catlin painted St. Louis in 1832. Bodmer the following year painted Fort Union, Fort Clark and Fort Pierre, while Miller has left us the best surviving views not only of the exterior but also the interior of Fort Laramie, both of which appear here.

[182]

A Creole Farm near St. Louis
By Anna Maria von Phul. About 1818

"The French of this country have their characteristic national manners, and are the same gay and happy people. Those among them that have standing, wealth, and education, show no other differences of character from the same classes of other nations, except such as result from their national temperament and manners. The poorer French have an unique and peculiar character. They were born in the woods or at least, far from society. They have been accustomed from infancy rather to the life of huntsmen, trappers, and boatmen, than of husbandmen. They generally make indifferent farmers. Their cabin, indeed, shows well at a distance, and the mud daubing is carefully white washed. They have gardens neatly laid out, and kept clean of weeds. Beyond this, the establishments of the *petits paysans* are generally sterile and comfortless."

Timothy Flint, *The History and Geography of the Mississippi Valley* (1831)

A Corner of St. Louis by the River
BY ANNA MARIA VON PHUL. 1818

"It may be questioned, whether the poorest class has been benefitted by the change [the Louisiana Purchase]. . . . Fearless of absolute want, they always lived in a careless and thoughtless manner: at present the greater part of them obtain a precarious subsistence. They generally possess a cart, a house or two, a small stock of cattle, and cultivate some spots of ground. At St. Louis they have more employment than in other villages; they make hay in the prairies, haul wood for sale, and are employed to do trifling jobs in town; some are boatmen or patrons."

H. M. Brackenridge, *Views of Louisiana* (1814)

[184]

Fort Laramie
BY ALFRED JACOB MILLER. 1837

"This post was built by the American Fur Co. situated about 800 miles West of St. Louis, is of a quadrangular form, with bastions at the diagonal corners to sweep the fronts in case of attack; over the ground entrance is a large block house, or tower, in which is placed a cannon. The interior is possibly 150 feet square, a range of houses built against the palisades entirely surround it, each apartment having a door and window overlooking the interior court. Tribes of Indians encamp here 3 or 4 times a year, bringing with them peltries to be traded or exchanged for dry-goods, tobacco, vermillion, brass, and diluted alcohol. Fontenel was in command of the fort, and received us with kindness and hospitality. We noticed around his apartment some large first-class engravings, from which we drew conclusions most favorable to Mr. F."

Alfred Jacob Miller, *Notes* (1837) quoted in *The West of Alfred Jacob Miller*, edited by Marvin C. Ross, 1951.

"Webster presents an interesting picture of conditions at Fort Laramie where a three-day halt . . . was made. The camping grounds near the fort were 'literally covered with wagon irons, clothing, beans, bacon, pork and provisions of almost all kinds, which have been left by the advance immigration to lighten their load and facilitate their speed.' Here, too, the Boston party abandoned the trunks which they had carried mule-back for 700 miles, and whose burden had done much to wear down the mules and ruin their backs."

Reuben Cole Shaw, *Across the Plains in Forty-nine* (1896)

[185]

Interior of Fort Laramie
By Alfred Jacob Miller. 1837

"The view is from the great entrance looking West, and embraces more than half the Court, or area. When this space is filled with Indians and Traders as it is at slated periods, the scene is lively and interesting. They gather here from all quarters. From the Gila at the South, the Red River at the North, and the Columbia River West, each has its quota and representatives. Siouxs, Bannocks, Mandans, Crows, Snakes, Peud-Orielles, Nez Perces, Cheyennes, and Delawares, —all except the Blackfeet, who are *bête noirs* and considered *de trop*. As a contrast, there are Canadian Trappers, free and otherwise, Half breeds, Kentuckians, Missourians, and Down Easters. A Saturnalia is held the first day and some excesses committed. But after this trading goes briskly forward.

"There was a cannon or two sleeping in the towers over the two main entrances, —the Indians having an aversion to their being wakened, entertaining a superstitious reverence for them. They are intended to keep the peace. This fort was built by Robert Campbell who named it Fort William in honor of his friend and partner Wm. Sublette. These gentlemen were the earliest pioneers after Messors Lewis and Clarke, and had many battles with the Indians. . . . We had almost daily intercourse with Sublette, Campbell, and Gov. Clarke in St. Louis, before we started."

Alfred Jacob Miller, *Notes* (1837), quoted in *The West of Alfred Jacob Miller*, edited by Marvin C. Ross, 1951

[218]

Fort Clark

Aquatint after a drawing by Charles Bodmer. 1839

"Arrived at the Mandan Village this morning at 7. The village is now occupied by the Ricarees old enemies of the Mandans, the latter having been obliged to succomb since their fearful reduction by the Small Pox, they have retired two or three miles further up the river, and are now considered as incorporated in the nation of the conquerors. The day has proved most unfortunate for our visit, a cold northeast wind and rain pouring down nearly the whole day. Notwithstanding, as this is our only day here, we determined to see all we could and walked up to the Fort [Fort Clark] and procured us an Indian Guide who took us to the Medicine Lodge and into his own lodge where we partook of the hospitality of the inmates by taking their mush. We certainly paid our visit under very unfavorable circumstances, not at all calculated to draw from us so bright a picture as our illustrious predecessor, Catlin, has given to this place. We all came to the conclusion that it was one of the dirtiest places we had ever seen human beings congregate in. The lodges are pretty much as he described them in a circular form & all covered with earth, and they are built so close together that there is barely room for two persons to pass between them and pick their way among the filth. In spite of the cold and storm these kindly sons of the prairies were shoeless, breechless and shirtless, the universal Buffalo robe being their only covering, and that generally thrown gracefully into their lap when they are seated."

Up the Missouri with Audubon. Journal of Edward Harris (1843), edited by John Francis McDermott, 1951

[187]

Fort Pierre

AQUATINT AFTER A DRAWING BY CHARLES BODMER. 1839

"Fort Pièrre was in excellent condition. The whole surrounding plain was covered with scattered tents of the Sioux, mostly of the Teton branch, and a few Yanktonans. Mr. Laidlow very kindly accommodated us, and assigned to us a spacious dwelling; I caused my boat to be unladen, as it was hinted that the vicinity of the half-starved Indians might prove dangerous to my bears. We found Fort Pièrre in great want of fresh provisions, no buffaloes having been seen during the whole winter, and the inmates of the fort, as well as the Indians, being very numerous. . . . For his own table, consisting of ten or twelve persons, Mr. Laidlow had generally bought dogs of the Indians, but these were now scarce, and consequently very dear: twelve dollars were paid for the dog destined for our repast to-day. There were, however, many superior provisions in the fort, which we enjoyed at Mr. Laidlow's table, after having long been deprived of them: one of these luxuries was new wheaten bread, and there were also potatoes, cabbages, carrots, several kinds of preserves and pickles, as well as coffee, sugar, tea, &c. I found here, also a part of my stock of provisions which I had brought from St. Louis last year, such as coffee, sugar, brandy, candles, &c., which would have been invaluable to me at Fort Clarke. The brandy had, however, been almost exhausted, and the cask filled up with water."

Maximilian, Prince of Wied, *Travels in the Interior of North America* (1843)

[188]

View of St. Louis

LITHOGRAPH AFTER A PAINTING BY J. C. WILD. About 1841

"The finest point from which to view the little 'City of the French' is from beneath the enormous sycamores upon the opposite bank of the Mississippi. It is from this spot alone that anything approaching to a cosmorama can be commanded. The city, retreating as it does from the river's brink—its buildings of every diversity of form, material, and structure, promiscuously heaped the one upon the other, and the whole intermingled with the fresh green of forest-trees, may boast of much scenic beauty. The range of white limestone warehouses, circling like a crescent the shore, form the most prominent feature of the foreground, while the forest of shruboaks sweeps away in the rear. For some time I gazed upon this imposing view, and then, slowly turning my horse's head, was upon the dusty thoroughfare to Edwardsville."

Edmund Flagg, *The Far West* (1838)

Fort Snelling
By J. C. WILD. 1844

"The spot which it is proposed to fortify is a high bluff at the junction of the River St. Peters with the Mississippi—a spot which commands the navigation of both rivers, and appears capable of being rendered impregnable with little expense. It is in fact the same point of land which first suggested to Lt. Pike the idea of its being an eligible situation for a fort and led to its subsequent purchase from the Sioux Indians. This purchase was effected at a treaty held by Lt. Pike in September 1805."

Henry R. Schoolcraft, *Narrative Journal of Travels in the Year 1820* (1821)

"About 50 years ago, an Indian camp stood on the bluff, now occupied by Fort Snelling . . . The Indian wigwams are now replaced by a well built fort, where the soldiers cultivate a farm for supplying the garrison with food. The whistle of the steamboat as she passes from Mendota to the Fort is heard instead of the cry of the painted warrior. The fort has a half crown battery fronting the river. The top of the bastions commands an extensive and imposing prospect.

"The scenery around Fort Snelling, which is situated on a high limestone bluff, near the confluence of the St. Peter's with the Mississippi River, is of a sublime and impressive character. Huge slabs of rock in the bed of the river and the towering cliffs on either side, reveal the existence of a mighty cataract in a remote age of the world, of which the receding Falls of St. Anthony now present only the diminished remains."

Charles A. Dana, editor, *The United States Illustrated* (1853)

St. Charles, Missouri

LITHOGRAPH BY A. JANICKE AND COMPANY. About 1850

"St. Charles was founded in 1780, and is situated on the left bank of the Missouri, about twenty-four miles above its mouth. It contains only one street, which extends upwards of a mile on the river, and is lined by about one hundred houses. The banks of the river along the town are not of a firm texture, and encroachments are apprehended. Owing to a hill, which extends along in the rear of the town, and nearly the whole length of it, the streets cannot be multiplied, nor any buildings erected, except on the borders of the present street. This village is remarkable for the health enjoyed by the inhabitants of it. Health, indeed, is more generally experienced on the Missouri than on any other of the rivers; and perhaps this results from the rapidity of its current, and from the cold and lively nature of its water, added to the nitrous and sulphureous qualities it contains."

Amos Stoddard, *Sketches, Historical and Descriptive of Louisiana* (1812)

"Next morning we reached St. Charles, on the N.E. shore, one of the oldest French settlements on the Missouri, consisting of about 300 houses, where the massive church, with its low tower, has a very good appearance. The environs of this scattered village are rather bare, but there were many European fruit trees in blossom. Most of the houses are built of wood, but a modern part of the place is of brick. On an eminence rising behind it, stands an old stone tower, which formerly served as a defense against the Indians."

Maximilian, Prince of Wied, *Travels in the Interior of North America* (1843)

[223]

Independence—Courthouse, Missouri
LITHOGRAPH PUBLISHED BY HERMANN J. MEYER. 1853

"The town of Independence was full of promise, like most of the innumerable towns springing up in the midst of the forests in the West, many of which, though dignified by high-sounding epithets, consist of nothing but a ragged congeries of five or six rough log-huts, two or three clap-board houses, two or three so-called hotels, alias grogshops; a few stores, a bank, printing office, and barn-looking church. It lacked, at the time I commemorate, the three last edifices, but was nevertheless a thriving and aspiring place, in its way; and the fortune made here already in the course of its brief existence, by a bold Yankee shopkeeper who sold sixty thousand dollars' worth of goods here in three years,—was a matter of equal notoriety, surprise, and envy. It is situated about twenty miles east of the Kansas River, and three miles south of the Missouri, and was consequently very near the extreme western frontier of the State. A little beyond this point, all carriage roads ceased, and one deep black trail alone, which might be seen tending to the southwest, was that of the Santa Fe trappers and traders."

Charles J. Latrobe, *The Rambler in North America 1832-33* (1836)

Weston, Missouri

BY AN UNKNOWN ARTIST. About 1853

"This rapidly growing town is on the left bank of the Missouri River, at a short bend, in the County of Platte. When the state of Missouri was first organized, the western boundary extended due north and south from the embouchure of the Kansas River . . . Weston is one of the principal landings on the Missouri, about forty miles above the mouth of the Kansas, and five miles above Fort Leavenworth, a military station on the right bank in the Indian territory. This is another place of outset and departure for the Californian, Oregon, and other western immigrants. . . . There is a bend in the river in front of the town. The landing is an excellent one and the harbour deep and commodious."

Charles A. Dana, editor, *The United States Illustrated* (1853)

[193]

Carondelet
BY HENRY LEWIS. 1854-58

"Carondelet is a picturesquely situated small French village. It lies about six miles from St. Louis, Missouri, and was founded in 1767 by the Frenchman Delor Detergette; thus it is approximately the same age as St. Louis. Many others followed the example of Delor, who first settled here; as they were not overloaded with worldly goods, whenever they came to St. Louis they were customarily met with the greeting by their friends: 'Here come the empty-pocket boys' ('*Voila les poches vides qui viennent!*'). This nickname of 'The empty-pocket boys' they answered by calling the city of St. Louis 'Short o'bread' ('*Pain court*'), since the city often suffered from famine.

"The village retained the nickname 'Empty pocket' until the year 1776, when it was officially named for the then governor of Louisiana, Carondelet. In recent times several solid brick buildings have been erected which greatly contrast with the delapidated frame structures of the first French settlers. Directly above the shore of the river there rises an enormous bluff, which is similar to that at Selma, and on the top of which one can see a number of handsome dwellings. . . .

"The inhabitants have many habits and customs in common with the Indians, with whom they have long associated, and have close relations. Their speech is a *patois* of French and Indian, which only they can understand."

George B. Douglas and Henry Lewis, *Das Illustrirte Mississippithal* (1854-58)

[226]

View of St. Louis from Lucas Place

LITHOGRAPH BY E. SACHSE AND COMPANY, BALTIMORE. About 1855-60

"St. Louis was also a point in the westward journey of emigrants and traders, and the current of these was ceaseless and unbroken. Here they purchased their supplies, as did the numerous caravans or expeditions proceeding across the plains to New Mexico, Utah, and California. Speculators of every kind hovered about the hotels and public places, and were as ardent in their dreams and seductive in their manners as so many oiley Gammons. The prairies for ten miles in every direction were laid out on paper in streets, avenues, and parks, and while St. Louis was in reality a fine and prosperous city, it was on paper and in the imagination of its inhabitants a much grander and more opulent place still, recalling Tom Moore's lines upon the Federal city, written in his anti-republican days:

> 'This famed metropolis, where fancy sees
> Squares in morasses, obelisks in trees.' "

John Lewis Peyton, *Over the Alleghanies and Across the Prairies* (1869)

[195]

Washington, Missouri

Lithograph after a drawing by Eduard Robyn. About 1860

"After seeing Mr. Fremont off in the fall of '53, I found the river so low that I left the boat which had brought me from Independence, and got off at Washington to go down by land.

". . . The clerk of the boat had told me there were only Germans there, and no communication with the railway, which was then finished only to a point twenty-seven miles lower down. . . .

"I spoke to a fatherly-looking man, to whom I explained that the river was low, and I was anxious to get to St. Louis immediately, and asked to be shown the way to the Hotel. In a very grave and silent way he turned up the bank, signing me to follow, which I did, a little troubled, but much more amused by the whole crowd following in solemn silence. If it had been an American town, all the necessary, and some unnecessary, questions would have been asked and answered in the first five minutes. But we made our way up the hill and into the clean, but ugly, comfortable town, and I was shown into the 'best room' of a large house, whose mistress and daughter came forward and made me as quietly welcome as though they knew me. Their faces, the furniture, the violins and guitar, and high pile of music-books; the pretty bright light hair of the women, too-tightly-plaited, all were Germany itself."

Jessie Benton Fremont, *The Story of the Guard* (1863)

[196]

Hermann, Missouri
LITHOGRAPH AFTER A DRAWING BY EDUARD ROBYN. About 1860

"But the wave of immigration, now that slavery was dead, had already reached her, and we found its healthful currents everywhere overflowing her bottoms and prairies. The new-comers seemed to be largely Yankee and German, almost everywhere. France once so predominant here, was already supplanted by Germany, and the Teuton bade fair to rule Missouri soon, even then. At Hermann, where we stopped for dinner, a German Hebe tendered us excellent native wine, and the culture of the grape, we learned, had already become a leading industry of this section of the state. The sturdy Rhine-men, as true to freedom as in the days of Tacitus, were already planting vineyards, and in the near future were sure of handsome returns from petty farms, that our old-time 'Pikes' and 'Border Ruffians' would have starved on."

James F. Rusling, *Across America* (1874)

"The history of the settlement of Hermann by the Germans is particularly interesting. The movement resulting in the selection of this location was originally under the auspices of the German Settlement Society of Philadelphia. The first meeting of this society of which any record is to be found at Hermann occurred June 10, 1836, for the purpose of considering the project of founding a German town."

History of Gasconade County (1888)

[197]

New Orleans from St. Patrick's Church
LITHOGRAPH AFTER A DRAWING BY J. W. HILL. 1852

"Not quite one hundred miles from the meeting of the Mississippi's turbid flood with the uncertain billows of the Mexican gulf is situated New Orleans—the Crescent City. Crescent in the shape of its waterfront and crescent in its advance and prosperity. Not quite a hundred miles from the union of river water and gulf waves, there advanced the Prow of LaSalle, the discoverer, a hundred and seventy-one years ago, to enable that gallant voyager to take possession of land 'in the name of the most puissant, most holy, most invincible and victorious Prince Louis, the Great King of France.'

"The city is difficult to describe, and difficult to write about. It must be seen to be known; so different are its complexion and ways from the other American cities. . . .

"The streets are quite straight and stretch over a thin layer of soil which the laborer's spade, at three to four feet through, breaks into water. The foundations of the high buildings are rather broad than deep and cellars are unknown.

"The first section of the city may be said to form a mile square and is thickly studded with buildings. . . . The younger portion of the metropolis shows the steeples which are always raised where saxon architects go."

Charles A. Dana, editor, *The United States Illustrated* (1853)

City of Burlington, Iowa
LITHOGRAPH AFTER A DRAWING BY W. BOURNE. 1858

"Those who made the first settlement [in Burlington] probably builded better than they knew, when they chose the only landing on the west bank of the Mississippi River, between New Madison and Muscatine, a distance of eighty-one miles. . . .

"Burlington is well situated for becoming a great commercial and manufacturing city—with lines of railroad radiating in every direction, bringing to her warehouses the products of near and distant portions of the country; with the Mississippi River at her door ready to float upon its bosom such products as seek a Southern market . . . it does appear as if a promising future opened before the city . . . ."

The History of Des Moines County, Iowa (1879)

"*Burlington*, the county seat, where the business capital of the county is mostly concentrated, and which also enjoys one of the most reliable rail road lines, (the Chicago & Burlington) as an eastern outlet, and an equally reliable line of freight and passenger boats for the north and south. These, with its numerous and varied manufacturing establishments, its extensive wholesale and retail dry goods and grocery stores, could not fail to make it not only the great trading town of the county but for several of the counties north and west, as well as for a large slice of Illinois lying opposite to it. Its population is about 12,000, and its public and private schools, and the character of its church edifices as well as its private dwellings, will compare favorably with any western city."

William Duane Wilson, *A Description of Iowa and Its Resources* (1865)

City of Davenport, Iowa
LITHOGRAPH AFTER A DRAWING BY RUFUS WRIGHT. About 1857-58

"We had a glimpse at Davenport, which is another beautiful city, crowning a hill—a phrase which applies to all these towns; for they are all comely, all well built, clean, orderly, pleasant to the eye, and cheering to the spirit; and they are all situated upon hills. Therefore we will give that phrase a rest. The Indians have a tradition that Marquette and Joliet camped where Davenport now stands, in 1673. The next white man who camped there, did it about a hundred and seventy years later—in 1834. Davenport has gathered its thirty thousand people within the past thirty years. She sends more children to her schools now than her whole population numbered twenty-three years ago. She has the usual Upper-River quota of factories, newspapers, and institutions of learning; she has telephones, local telegraphs, an electric alarm, and an admirable paid fire department, consisting of six hook and ladder companies, four steam fire-engines, and thirty churches. Davenport is the official residence of two bishops—Episcopal and Catholic.

"Opposite Davenport is the flourishing town of Rock Island, which lies at the foot of the Upper Rapids. A great railroad bridge connects the two towns—one of the thirteen which fret the Mississippi and the pilots between St. Louis and St. Paul."

Mark Twain, *Life on the Mississippi* (1874)

Des Moines, Iowa, From the Capitol
LITHOGRAPH AFTER A DRAWING BY G. L. REYNOLDS. 1858

". . . The original town of Fort Des Moines was laid out in June, 1846. But its extent as then specified, comprises but a small portion of the present limits of our city. Its streets and squares have extended in all directions, and manifold additions have been made to the original plat, both west and east of the Des Moines river.

"That part of the city east of the Des Moines, and formerly called East Fort Des Moines, was not, under the town charter, included within the corporation, but the city charter comprises both sides of the river. The eastern side is not so favorable, by nature, for a town site, as the western. The space between the river and the adjacent hills is narrower, and a considerable portion of the valley is low and subject, in time of high water, to be partly overflowed. There is a level stretch of ground near the bluffs that is higher, and were it sufficiently extensive would constitute an admirable site for a town. Still, buildings are being erected throughout the whole bottom, on the slope of the hill where the Capitol is located, and even beyond it. The whole hill side and valley, from present appearances, will in a few years be entirely covered with houses. Some of those now erected are very fine and costly.

"On the brows of the surrounding eminences are many very beautiful situations for suburban residences, commanding a view of the entire city, and the Des Moines and its tributary winding around it like belts of glistening silver. On one of the most commanding of these knolls the Capital Building is placed."

H. B. Turrill, *Historical Reminiscences of the City of Des Moines* (1857)

Herndon Hotel, Omaha, Nebraska
BY F. HAKLHUBER. About 1860

"The main street, Farnham Street, connected this business section with the bank of the river. On this street there were two or three half blocks of brick houses, a number of shops built of planks, as many bars and eating houses of low quality, ending in the Herndon Hotel on the edge of the plateau above the high-water mark of the Missouri. There the street becomes a mere trail and plunges through an opening in the encampment down the slope, across the tracks by the depot of the Pacific Railroad to the bank of the river."

Philippe Régis de Trobriand, *Military Life in Dakota* (1867-1869), edited by Lucile M. Kane, 1951

Omaha, Nebraska
LITHOGRAPH AFTER A DRAWING BY LEWIS KURZ. 1868

"The initial point of the railway is, as I remarked in my previous letter at Omaha, Nebraska, a city which has sprung into existence on the right bank of the Missouri river, since 1856, near the 41st degree of north latitude, and now containing a population of 10,000 souls. The streets and avenues are wide and handsomely built, and the mansions, warehouses, storerooms, and shops are generally constructed of brick, and are of imposing size. The spot which was some years ago, the site of a solitary Indian wigwam, is now the seat of a flourishing trade and of many manufacturing establishments, which, though in their infancy, contribute largely to the substantial wealth and prosperity of the community."

John Lewis Peyton, *Over the Alleghanies and Across the Prairies* (1869)

[203]

Gulch Mine, Central City, Colorado
BY EMANUEL LEUTZE. 1861

"The gulch miner has been here in all his pristine strength and glory. Gravel, sand, bowlders, rocks—not one stone left upon another; not one where Nature put it. The entire bed of the stream in the condition of the Kentuckian who was 'uneasy in his mind'. It was all 'tore up'. Here sent as high up the bank as impossible hydraulics would allow, and left to feel and trickle its way along a steep mountain side some hundred feet below, that crowbar, pickaxe, and spade might hold high revel in its quiet bed; there put into the straight-jacket of a race, to feed that water-wheel now rotting like the dam above it. Old cradles, broken rockers, quartz pounders half completed and abandoned, a lonely grave or two up the hillside, requiemed over every night by the wild pines. Nothing more is left of the gulch miner, whose occasional prize of a nugget lured hundreds from happy homes and richer placers in their quiet fields. He has passed on. He is eighty or a hundred miles further west, close behind the trapper, whose quiet haunts he invaded."

J. F. Meline, *Two Thousand Miles on Horseback* (1867)

Pike's Peak and Colorado City
LITHOGRAPH AFTER A DRAWING BY A. E. MATHEWS. 1866

"Those whom we meet here coming down confirm the worst news we have had from the Peak. There is scarcely any gold there; those who dig cannot average two shillings per day; all who can get away are leaving; Denver and Auraria are nearly deserted; terrible sufferings have been endured on the Plains, and more must yet be encountered; hundreds would gladly work for their board, but cannot find employment—in short, Pike's Peak is an exploded bubble, which thousands must bitterly rue to the end of their days. Such is the tenor of our latest advices. I have received none this side of Leavenworth that contradict them. My informant says all are getting away who can, and that we shall find the region nearly deserted."

Horace Greeley, *An Overland Journey, from New York to San Francisco* (1860)

"Soon the sun rose bright and clear; but the air was keen, with a stiff breeze eastward in our teeth. We were down in a wide depression of the Plains; but presently we rose up out of it, and as we struck the summit of the 'divide,' lo, the Rocky Mountains were before us in all their grandeur and sublimity. To the north rose Long's Peak, fourteen thousand feet above the sea, heaven-kissing, but with his night-cap still on; to the south, was Pike's Peak, eleven thousand feet above the sea, snow-crowned; while between, a hundred miles or more, swelled and towered the Mountains—at the base mere foot-hills, then ridge mounting on ridge and peak on peak, until over and above all the Snowy Range cropped out sublime."

James F. Rusling, *Across America* (1874)

Fort Arbuckle, Oklahoma Territory
BY VINCENT COLYER. 1868

"While I was stationed at Camp Arbuckle, on the Canadian River, in 1850, a band of prairie Indians came in to see us, and, as this was probably the first time they had ever entered a white man's habitation, every thing was novel to them, and their curiosity was very much excited. The chief examined various articles of furniture, books, and pictures, but nothing seemed to attract his attention so much as an oil-cloth rug upon the floor. It was covered with bright colors, which appeared to take his fancy amazingly, and he scrutinized it very closely. He scraped it with his finger nails, and, wetting his fingers, tried to wash off the coloring; and, after he had seen all that interested him, inquired if the President had sent me all those things from Washington. My wife showed him specimens of embroidery, which pleased him so much that he paid her the compliment of proposing to exchange wives with me, and, upon my referring him to her for a decision, he informed me that he was not in the habit of trading with squaws, but if I would only say the word, he was ready to swap right off . . . .

"Our little army, scattered as it has been over the vast area of our possessions, in small garrisons of one or two companies each, has seldom been in a situation to act successfully on the offensive against large numbers of these marauders, and has often been condemned to hold itself almost exclusively upon the defensive. The morale of the troops must thereby necessarily be seriously impaired, and the confidence of the savages correspondingly augmented. The system of small garrisons has a tendency to disorganize the troops in proportion as they are scattered, and renders them correspondingly inefficient."

Randolph B. Marcy, *Thirty Years of Army Life on the Border* (1866)

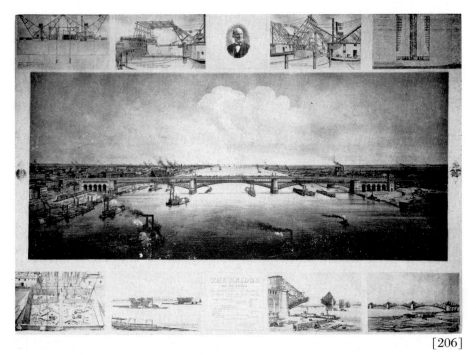

[206]

The Bridge at St. Louis
Lithograph Published by Compton and Company, St. Louis. 1874

"The towboat and the railroad had done their work, and done it well and completely. The mighty bridge, stretching along over our heads, had done its share in the slaughter and spoliation. Remains of former steamboatmen told me, with wan satisfaction, that the bridge doesn't pay. Still, it can be no sufficient compensation to a corpse to know that the dynamite that laid him out was not of as good quality as it had been supposed to be."

Mark Twain, *Life on the Mississippi* (1874)

The Eads Bridge, a masterpiece of engineering and architectural design, was built in 1872. It was the work of Captain James B. Eads, and signalized the beginning of the end of the great age of steamboat navigation on the Mississippi.

[207]

St. Paul, Minnesota
LITHOGRAPH AFTER A DRAWING BY GEORGE H. ELLSBURY. 1874

"St. Paul's was a small settlement at the Falls of the Mississippi which had grown up around the United States' garrison, and was distinguished for nothing but its frontier appearance and the discomforts to which adventurous travellers, who found their way here, must submit. A sagacious down-easter, Mr. Cook, understanding the advantages of the place at the head of steam-boat navigation and foreseeing its future importance, established himself on the spot, built the house in which we were now guests, and opened an hotel. He had also 'entered' a considerable body of land, which he divided into squares, these were subdivided into town lots, and he was selling them at a high price to such strangers as followed into the country. . . .

"Nevertheless, the prospect of having a railway at some day, however remote, exercised no small influence on the price of town lots. In their office I listened to many edifying conversations upon the subject of the new buildings, which were in a twelvemonth to grace the city; and began to have confused ideas of Gothic windows, Palladian attics, Bysantine arches, Rococo facades and Tudor chimneys floating promiscuously through my mind. . . .

"It would be difficult to imagine a more beautiful country than that around St. Paul's, or a more advantageous situation for a town."

John Lewis Peyton, *Over the Alleghanies and Across the Prairies* (1869)

Minneapolis, Minnesota

LITHOGRAPH AFTER A DRAWING BY A. RUGER. 1879

"Minneapolis is situated at the falls of St. Anthony, which stretch across the river fifteen hundred feet, and have a fall of eight-two feet—a waterpower which, by art, has been made of inestimable value, businesswise, though somewhat to the damage of the Falls as a spectacle, or as a background against which to get your photograph taken.

"Thirty flouring-mills turn out two million barrels of the very choicest of flour every year; twenty saw-mills produce two hundred million feet of lumber annually; then there are woolen-mills, cotton-mills, paper and oil mills; and sash, nail, furniture, barrel, and other factories, without number, so to speak. The great flouring-mills here and at St. Paul use the 'new process' and mash the wheat by rolling, instead of grinding it.

"Sixteen railroads meet in Minneapolis, and sixty-five passenger-trains arrive and depart daily.

"In this place, as in St. Paul, journalism thrives. Here there are three great dailies, ten weeklies, and three monthlies.

"There is a university, with four hundred students—and, better still, its good efforts are not confined to enlightening the one sex. There are sixteen public schools, with buildings which cost five hundred thousand dollars; there are six thousand pupils and one hundred and twenty-eight teachers. There are also seventy churches existing, and a lot more projected. The banks aggregate a capital of three million dollars, and the wholesale jobbing trade of the town amounts to fifty million dollars a year."

Mark Twain, *Life on the Mississippi* (1874)

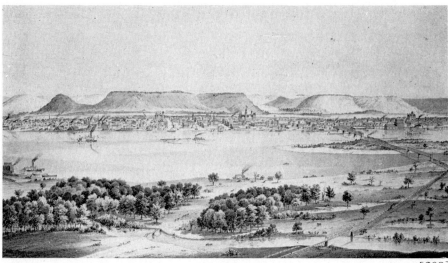

[209]

Winona, Minnesota

LITHOGRAPH AFTER A DRAWING BY GEORGE ELLSBURY AND VERNON GREEN. 1874

"Having reached the Minnesota side of the river we rushed along toward Winona our evening destination where we had supper and remained for the night . . . . The growth of Winona since my former visit has been gradual and substantial. Several new public buildings were noted in various parts of the city of which her intelligent citizens are justly proud.

"In its location and surroundings, Winona is extremely picturesque, standing as it does on a plateau nine miles long by three broad on the west bank of the river, and environed by lofty bluffs, the surface of which in some cases, from base to summit appears of a velvety smoothness, having more the semblance of art than of nature.

"The city is laid out with the utmost regularity, the streets wide and chiefly at right angles; the business blocks compactly built of wood and stone are generally of a very substantial character."

Willard Glazier, *Headwaters of the Mississippi* (1893)

Red Wing, Minnesota
LITHOGRAPH AFTER A DRAWING BY GEORGE I. RICHARDS. 1874

"Half a mile east of Red Wing's village there is an isolated mountain standing upon the brink of the river, called the Grange, from the summit of which you enjoy the most charming prospect. The immense valley of the Mississippi with the numerous channels and islands of the river—the prairies, and the forests— with the windings of a number of small rivers which flow into the Mississippi, spread like a map below the eye."

Henry R. Schoolcraft, *Narrative Journal of Travels in the Year 1820* (1821)

"On the homeward journey from Mr. Lindholm's farm to St. Paul, we passed through the little town of Redwing, about 5,000 strong, so called after a famous Indian chief who is said to lie buried in a nearby mound. In this pretty little town on the Mississippi there are about 900 Swedes. Here we were invited to take part in a mid-summer picnic, which happened to be in progress at a farm owned by a Swede eight or ten English miles from town. Here again I met a large number of Swedes and became fully convinced of the good living conditions which all Swedes residing in this part of Minnesota enjoy. . . . Since this first visit I have been in Redwing several times and have joined in many excursions from that place, and I shall always preserve in grateful memory the heartfelt friendliness and hospitality which always was my lot there."

Hugo Nisbeth, *Two Years in America* (1874)

Fort Harker, Kansas
By Hermann Stieffel. 1879

"From Fort Riley we marched to Fort Harker, a distance of ninety miles, where our force was strengthened by the addition of two more troops of cavalry. . . .

"Fort Harker was established in 1864 on the Smoky Hill River, four miles southeast of present-day Ellsworth, Kansas. At first it was named Fort Ellsworth, the change to Fort Harker being made in 1866. In 1867 the fort was reestablished on a new site, about a mile distant from the old one. For years it was a shipping center for goods bound for New Mexican points. It was abandoned as a military establishment in April, 1872."

George A. Custer, *My Life on the Plains* (1874)

Miles City, Montana
By Hermann Stieffel. 1879

"Some years ago when living on his ranch ten miles above Coulson he was sub-poenaed to serve on the grand jury which was to meet at Miles City. A neighbor named William Rogers hearing that he was going to Miles called on him and requested permission to go with him. Mr. Allen gladly accepted his company and it was arranged that they should start early the next morning, and go down the river in a skiff. When they got all their traps on board it was discovered that neither of them had provided a gun, Mr. A's gun being out of order and Mr. R. having lately sold his. They talked the matter over and it looked like a risky place of business to start on a voyage like this of one hundred and fifty miles down the Yellowstone River, through a country where they were liable to be jumped by hostile reds, without a gun in the boat."

G. O. Shields, *Rustlings in the Rockies* (1883)

"Miles City stands on the east bank of the Tongue River and in a grove of big cottonwood trees of which a great many have the bark torn from the upper side of them for several feet above the ground by an ice gorge here apparently about twelve or fifteen years ago, perhaps longer, so some day the town will likely be destroyed by another gorge—bad location . . . There is also a wire rope ferry across Tongue River at Miles City . . . The hotel accommodations in Miles City in 1880 were not first class, in fact I do not think there were any hotel accommodations."

Granville Stuart, *Forty Years on the Frontier* (1904)

[213]

Fort Keough, Montana
By Hermann Stieffel. 1879

"We passed through Miles City at half past ten and a few minutes later arrived at Fort Keough which is situated two miles further up the river . . . I proceeded at once to the quarters of my old friend, Captain Borden. . . . The next day being Sunday, we spent it in looking about the post and the city and in friendly intercourse with the various officers at the post."

G. O. Shields, *Rustlings in the Rockies* (1883)

Westward by Land and by Water

THE HISTORY of American expansion into the Louisiana Territory has left us two unmistakable symbols of the West, the covered wagon and the steamboat. And rightly so for they both symbolize movement. Yet by the close of the period covered by this survey, the steamboat and the covered wagon had given way to the iron highway of the steam engine. The joining of the rails of the Central Pacific and the Northern Pacific at Promontory Point in Utah in 1869 was one of the great events of the nineteenth century.

The artists' record of the role of the prairie schooner has been treated in the section on the white man as a phase of the individual pioneer's encounter with the West. The pages that follow deal with the scheduled transportation by boat and train that provided such important means for settling the great inland empire—establishing commerce between the Mississippi and the frontier a thousand miles to the West and carrying the emigrants to their new homes.

It is a curious fact that the stirring spectacle of this pageant of commerce inspired so few artists of distinction to make it a subject of their work. The contemporary record must be credited largely to printmakers and the artists they employed as a commercial enterprise.

Of the three artists represented in this section by paintings, one is unknown. Of the other two, Thomas Otter and Newbold H. Trotter, almost nothing is known save their names and the fact that they painted these pictures.

Steamer "Yellowstone"
AQUATINT AFTER A DRAWING BY CHARLES BODMER. 1839

"Our engine was broken, so that we could not proceed till the next morning (18th April [1833]). . . . After the people had returned on board, at the repeated summons of the bell, we proceeded on our voyage, but were soon obliged to take soundings, and to saw off some dangerous snags; we then landed twenty men on a sand bank, to tow the steamer, but their efforts broke the rope, and they all tumbled one upon another, to the great amusement of those on board. By way of precaution, our vessel was fastened to a large tree, which proved our safety, for the rudder was soon afterwards deranged, and rendered unserviceable. It was repaired about two o'clock, but we soon run aground on a sand bank, where we were obliged to remain all night, in a rather unsafe situation, for the current, on the bank, was very strong, and we could not fasten the vessel to anything, so that we might easily have been carried down the stream; the river, however, continued to subside. On the morning of the 19th a flat boat was procured, to lighten our vessel, by landing a part of the cargo, which was piled up in the wood, on the bank, and covered with cloths. Mr. Bodmer made a faithful sketch of this scene."

Maximilian, Prince of Wied, *Travels in the Interior of North America* (1843)

Steamboat Loading Passengers
BY AN UNKNOWN ARTIST. About 1840

"A stranger to this mode of travelling would find it difficult to describe his impressions upon descending the Mississippi for the first time in one of these steamboats, which we have named. He contemplates the prodigious construction, with its double tiers of cabins, and its separate establishment for the ladies, and its commodious arrangements for the deck passengers and the servants. Over head, about him, and below him, all is life and movement. He contemplates the splendor of the cabin, its beautiful finishing of the richest woods, its rich carpeting, its mirrors and fine furniture, its sliding tables, its bar room, and all its arrangements for the accommodation of a hundred cabin passengers. The fare is sumptuous, and everything in a style of splendor, order and quiet, far exceeding most city taverns. You read, converse, walk, or sleep, as you choose. You are not burdened by the restraint of useless ceremony. The varied and verdant scenery shifts about you. The trees, the green islands, the houses on the shore, everything has an appearance, as by enchantment, of moving past you."

Timothy Flint, *The History and Geography of the Mississippi Valley* (1831)

High Pressure Steamboat Mayflower
LITHOGRAPH AFTER A DRAWING BY C. H. PARSONS. 1855

"The moment we were under way I began to prowl about the great steamer and fill myself with joy. She was as clean and as dainty as a drawing-room; when I looked down her long, gilded saloon, it was like gazing through a splendid tunnel; she had an oil-picture, by some gifted sign-painter, on every stateroom door; she glittered with no end of prism-fringed chandeliers; the clerk's office was elegant, the bar was marvelous, and the barkeeper had been barbered and upholstered at incredible cost. The boiler-deck (i.e., the second story of the boat, so to speak) was as spacious as a church, it seemed to me; so with the forecastle; and there was no pitiful handful of deck-hands, firemen, and roustabouts down there, but a whole battalion of men. The fires were fiercely glaring from a long row of furnaces, and over them were eight huge boilers! This was unutterable pomp. . . .

"My chief was presently hired to go on a big New Orleans boat, and I packed my satchel and went with him. She was a grand affair. When I stood in her pilot-house I was so far above the water that I seemed perched on a mountain; and her decks stretched so far away, fore and aft, below me, that I wondered how I could ever have considered the little *Paul Jones* a large craft."

Mark Twain, *Life on the Mississippi* (1874)

Steamboats on the Mississippi
BY FRANCES F. PALMER. About 1860

"The Steam-Boats on the Mississippi, which are vessels from two to four hundred tons burden, are moved by one engine, generally on the high-pressure principle. As the water in which they have to navigate is always smooth, and the winds are seldom violent, they are enabled to adopt two very commodious devices, which it would be impossible to apply to sea-going steam-vessels. The deck is made to extend on both sides eight or ten feet beyond the hull, by which a great additional width is acquired, while over this wide space they are enabled to form two tiers of accommodations above the deck. In the lower range the usual luxuries of a packet are provided for passengers who require staterooms or sleeping berths; and those who have the means of paying for such entertainment have an ample table provided for them. There is in all these boats, also a separate cabin for the ladies in a third suite, which lies below the deck.

"The upper tier of all is occupied by what are called Deck Passengers, chiefly consisting of the men who, having floated down the Mississippi in their great flats or arks, take advantage of the steam-boats to return home again. These deck passengers, of course, pay a much smaller sum than those below stairs, as they provide themselves, and have but rough lodgings allotted them. They generally contract for an abatement of two dollars from their passage-money, on condition of assisting to carry on board the fire-wood; so that, for about eight dollars, or about £1, 14s., they are carried upwards of a thousand miles."

Basil Hall, *Forty Etchings, from Sketches made with the Camera Lucida, in North America* (1829)

Bound Down the River

LITHOGRAPH AFTER A PAINTING BY GEORGE F. FULLER. 1860

"Here, now, start that gang-plang fo'ard! Lively, now! *What*'re you about!
Snatch it! *snatch* it! There! there! After again! aft again! Don't you hear me?
Dash it to dash! are you going to *sleep* over it! '*Vast* heaving. 'Vast heaving,
I tell you! Going to heave it clear astern? *Where*'re you going with that barrel!
fo'ard with it 'fore I make you swallow it, you dash-dash-dash-*dashed* split be-
tween a tired mud-turtle and a crippled hearse-horse.' "

Mark Twain, *Life on the Mississippi* (1874)

On the Road
By Thomas Otter. About 1860

"If 1870 shall see the locomotive sweep from Omaha to San Francisco, 1871 should hear its shrill song reverberate over the plains and through the mountains from St. Paul to Puget Sound; and while the Central will be hastening its share of travel and freight across the New World, the growing tide of trade will sweep through these rich valleys until every nation shall pay tribute to the Northern Pacific Railroad. It will bring not only the matchless wealth of the new Northwest, but the commerce of the ancient empires will pass us as it seeks the Eastern cities and Europe toward the rising instead of the setting sun; and the crowning pride of the Republic will be this great artery of national and commercial life."

A. K. McClure, *Three Thousand Miles through the Rocky Mountains* (1869)

"The Pacific Railroad is stretching out its iron arm to the region of gold at the rate of a mile a day, ready to bring freight over precisely the worst part of the route for wagons. War is over; wood is growing on the spot. Every additional comer reduces the price of labor. Emigrants are coming in, and mines will be worked before next winter at one half the prices of 1865."

J. F. Meline, *Two Thousand Miles on Horseback* (1867)

Across the Continent: Westward the Course of Empire Takes its Way.
LITHOGRAPH AFTER A DRAWING BY FRANCES F. PALMER. 1868

"The difference between the number who would take an ocean steamer or a prairie waggon, and a modern American or palace car, with its luxurious state-rooms, where the traveller eats and sleeps almost as comfortably as at home, may be as great as the difference between the numbers who were jolted over the mountains in an old fashioned stage coach, and those in an express train between any two great cities. It may be safely said then that this *through* travel from ocean to ocean will be at once doubled upon the completion of the road in January 1, 1870, and with the rapid increase of the population on the Pacific in the next few years, more than quadrupled . . .

"You will see from these facts and statements that this railroad is not only destined to be a national work of the highest importance, and the source of the greatest wealth to its stockholders, but a public blessing to the people of both hemispheres.

"For the energy with which they have prosecuted this important work the Americans are, it must be allowed, entitled to every praise; every blow they strike upon it, is a blow struck in behalf of peaceful commerce and the trade of the world. It will not only subserve the interests of the United States' Government and people, but those of Asia, Australia, and Europe alike."

John Lewis Peyton, *Over the Alleghanies and Across the Prairies* (1869)

[221]

Locomotive Arkansas with Tender McKay of the Little Rock and Fort Smith Railway
LITHOGRAPH BY H. THOMAS AND D. DRUMMOND. About 1870

"Men of the East! Men at Washington! You have given the toil and even the blood of a million of your brothers and fellows for four years, and spent three thousand million dollars, to rescue one section of the Republic from barbarism and from anarchy; and your triumph makes the cost cheap. Lend now a few thousand of men, and a hundred millions of money, to create a new Republic; to marry to the Nation of the Atlantic an equal if not greater Nation of the Pacific. Anticipate a new sectionalism, a new strife, by a triumph of the arts of peace that shall be even prouder and more reaching than the victories of your Arms. Here is payment of your great debt; here is wealth unbounded; here the commerce of the world; here the completion of a Republic that is continental; but you must come and take them with the Locomotive!"

Samuel Bowles, *Across the Continent* (1865)

"The tourist who glides rapidly and with such keen enjoyment through this region, can scarcely conceive that but a few years have elapsed since it contained thousands of murderous savages; for it is a noteworthy fact that nothing so soon moderates the danger of Indian attacks as a railroad. It seems that, even if no fighting is done, the mere presence of the road, with daily passage of trains, either drives the Indians away or renders them harmless."

J. H. Beadle, *Western Wilds, and the Men Who Redeem Them* (1878)

[222]

Prairie Fires of the Great West
LITHOGRAPH PUBLISHED BY CURRIER AND IVES. 1871

"The event I alluded to yesterday was a great fire on the prairies, which was blown toward us by the wind and which we watched with anxiety. It first showed up in the afternoon, a drifting mass of smoke, which formed an enormous fawn-colored cloud blown along by a northwest wind. As the wind increased from one minute to the next, it was very difficult to estimate how far away the fire was. Nevertheless, it was evident even at the distance separating us from the fire that the extent of the blaze appeared to be considerable. In fact, when a strong wind lifted or parted the vast curtain of smoke which began to darken the sun, red, white, and brown columns could be clearly seen spiralling up on the horizon beyond the bluffs."

Philippe Régis de Trobriand, *Military Life in Dakota* (1867-1869), edited by Lucile M. Kane, 1951

"The year 1872 opened with a revival of interest in the Atlantic and Pacific Railroad, otherwise known as the Thirty-fifth Parallel Route. This road was already completed from St. Louis to Vinita, in the Indian Territory, and was to run thence westward to the Rio Grande, and through a succession of valleys and passes, nearly on the line of the thirty-fifth parallel, to California, terminating at San Francisco. That city and St. Louis had struck hands on the project; thirty-five million dollars had been pledged; it was the era of speculative railroad construction, and we were promised an early completion of the line."

J. H. Beadle, *Western Wilds, and the Men Who Redeem Them* (1878)

Fort Harker, Kansas
BY HERMANN STIEFFEL. 1879

"In all this part of Kansas, the Indian had already had his day, and everywhere was being fast eliminated. The valleys of the Kaw and its two chief tributaries, the Republican and Smoky Hill, had already heard the whistle of the white man's locomotive, and the whole region there was beginning to shake with the tread of the onward march of civilization. As 'Bleeding Kansas,' she had had her dark days; but these, happily, were past, and the tide wave of eastern immigration was now surging and swelling all up and down her borders. We met cheery voices and friendly hands at every stage of progress; and could not but bid Kansas a hearty God-speed as we journeyed on."

James F. Rusling, *Across America* (1874)

"Men and brethren! let us resolve to have a railroad to the Pacific—to have it soon. It will add more to the strength and wealth of our country than would the acquisition of a dozen Cubas. It will prove a bond of union not easily broken, and a new spring to our national industry, prosperity and wealth. It will call new manufactures into existence, and increase the demand for the products of those already existing. It will open new vistas to national and to individual aspiration, and crush out filibusterism by giving a new and wholesome direction to the public mind."

Horace Greeley, *An Overland Journey from New York to San Francisco* (1860)

Held Up

By N. H. Trotter. 1897

"Several of our party who passed over this route frequently, between 1851 and 1857, inform us that at that time, these immense plains, stretching in every direction around us, were covered with the buffalo—to such an extent, indeed, as frequently to impede the progress of trains. That vast numbers have been killed here is evident, for the road is a perfect buffalo Golgotha—or place of skulls—their short, thick, curved horns enabling you readily to distinguish their heads from those of the domestic ox."

J. F. Meline, *Two Thousand Miles on Horseback* (1867)

Lenders

Mrs. Francis P. Garvan, Roslyn, N.Y.; Mr. Everett D. Graff, Chicago; Mr. and Mrs. Edwin Grossman, St. Louis; Mr. Louis W. Hill, Jr., St. Paul; Mr. Robert B. Honeyman, Jr., Pasadena; Mr. Arthur Hoskins, St. Louis; Mr. Hall Park McCullough, North Bennington, Vt.; Mr. and Mrs. John F. Merriam, Omaha; Mr. and Mrs. J. Maxwell Moran, Malvern, Pa.; Mr. Claiborne Pell, Washington; Mrs. Clyde H. Porter, Kansas City; Mr. Claude J. Ranney, Malvern, Pa.; Mr. Ernest R. Reiff, North St. Paul; Mr. Henry Schnakenberg, Newton, Conn.; Mr. Frank H. Shaffer, Jr., Cincinnati; Mr. A. Howard Stebbins, Jr., Little Rock; Mr. Bronson Trevor, New York.

The American Museum of Natural History, New York; Art Museum of the New Britain Institute, New Britain, Conn.; The Berkshire Museum, Pittsfield, Mass.; The Boatmen's National Bank of St. Louis; The Brooklyn Museum; The Butler Institute of American Art, Youngstown, O.; The Century Association, New York; Chicago Historical Society; City Art Museum of St. Louis; The Corcoran Gallery of Art, Washington; Davenport Public Museum; The Detroit Institute of Arts; Harvard University, Cambridge; James Jerome Hill Reference Library, St. Paul; Kunstmuseum, Basel, Switzerland; Kunstverein, Solothurn, Switzerland; Mercantile Library, St. Louis; Minnesota Historical Society, St. Paul; Missouri Historical Society, St. Louis; Museum of Fine Arts, Boston; The Museum of Fine Arts of Houston; Newark Museum, Newark, N.J.; The Public Library, Denver, Colo.; Schloss Neuwied, Germany; Smithsonian Institution, Washington; The Union League Club, New York; Wadsworth Atheneum, Hartford, Conn.; The Walters Art Gallery, Baltimore; Washington University, St. Louis; William Rockhill Nelson Gallery of Art, Kansas City; Yale University, New Haven.

Edward Eberstadt and Sons, New York; Kennedy Galleries, Inc., New York; M. Knoedler and Company, New York; The Old Print Shop, Inc., New York; Mr. Victor D. Spark, New York.

Catalogue

THE LAND: RIVER, PLAIN AND MOUNTAIN

SEYMOUR, SAMUEL

[1]
Cliffs of Red Sandstone near the Rocky Mountains, watercolor, 8½" x 10⅝". Collection William Robertson Coe, Yale University Library.

[2]
View of the Arkansas near the Rocky Mountains, watercolor, 8½" x 10⅝". Collection William Robertson Coe, Yale University Library.

WÜRTTEMBERG, PRINCE PAUL of

[3]
View of the Missouri at Wasa-bae Wak-anda-ge, colored lithograph, 11¾" x 16½". Collection City Art Museum of St. Louis.

CATLIN, GEORGE

[4]
Prairie Fire, oil, 11" x 14¼". Collection Smithsonian Institution, Washington.

BODMER, CHARLES

[5]
Cliffs on the Upper Missouri, watercolor, 5¼" x 7¾". Collection Schloss Neuwied, Germany. Courtesy Prinz Dietrich zu Wied.

[6]
Curious Formations on the Upper Missouri, watercolor, 8" x 12½". Collection Schloss Neuwied, Germany. Courtesy Prinz Dietrich zu Wied.

[7]
Snags on the Missouri, colored aquatint, 15⅝" x 21¼". Collection City Art Museum of St. Louis.

[8]
Confluence of the Yellowstone and Missouri Rivers, colored aquatint, 22" x 25½". Collection James Jerome Hill Reference Library, St. Paul.

MILLER, ALFRED JACOB

[9]
Prairie, watercolor, 9" x 11¾". Collection Mrs. Clyde H. Porter, Kansas City.

[10]
Scott's Bluff near the Platte, watercolor, 7" x 18¾". Collection Mrs. Clyde H. Porter, Kansas City.

[11]
The Devil's Gate, watercolor, 7" x 10". Collection Edward Eberstadt and Sons, New York.

[12]
Lake Scene. Wind River Mountains, watercolor, 10" x 12½". Collection Mrs. Clyde H. Porter, Kansas City.

UNKNOWN ARTIST

[13]
High Water in the Bayou Country, watercolor, 8⅝" x 11⅞". Collection City Art Museum of St. Louis.

WILD, JOHN CASPER

[14]
View of Davenport, Iowa, and the Mississippi, watercolor, 22" x 34". Collection Davenport Public Museum.

[15]
Dubuque, Iowa, colored lithograph, 21¾" x 30¾". Collection Chicago Historical Society.

EASTMAN, SETH

[16]
The Laughing Waters, watercolor, 13⅛" x 16⅛". Collection James Jerome Hill Reference Library, St. Paul.

[17]
Falls of St. Anthony, watercolor, 13⅛" x 16⅛". Collection James Jerome Hill Reference Library, St. Paul.

BINGHAM, GEORGE CALEB

[18]
The Storm, oil, 25" x 30". Collection Wadsworth Atheneum, Hartford. Gift of Henry Schnakenberg.

STANLEY, JOHN MIX

[19]
Western Landscape, oil, 18½" x 30". Collection The Detroit Institute of Arts.

BIERSTADT, ALBERT

[20]
Mountain Lake, oil, 36" x 52". Collection The Museum of Fine Arts, Houston.

[21]
Western Sunset, oil, 32" x 48". Collection Bronson Trevor, New York.

[22]
Jenny Lake, Wyoming, oil, 30" x 44". Collection Edward Eberstadt and Sons, New York.

[23]
Wind River Country, Wyoming, oil, 26½" x 40½". Collection Art Museum of the New Britain Institute, New Britain, Connecticut.

WIMAR, CHARLES

[24]
Cottonwoods on the Missouri, drawing, 9⅞" x 15¼." Collection Missouri Historical Society, St. Louis.

[25]
White Castles on the Missouri, drawing, 9¾" x 15". Collection Missouri Historical Society, St. Louis.

[26]
Buttes on the Missouri, drawing, 9¾" x 15¼". Collection Missouri Historical Society, St. Louis.

MORAN, THOMAS

[27]
Western Landscape, oil, 29" x 44". Collection Art Museum of the New Britain Institute, New Britain, Connecticut.

BUCHSER, FRANK

[28]
On the Platte, oil, 9⅝" x 16¾". Collection Kunstmuseum, Basel, Switzerland.

[29]
The Lonesome Rider, oil, 16⅝" x 24⅞". Collection Kunstmuseum, Basel, Switzerland.

WHITTREDGE, WORTHINGTON

[30]
In the Rockies, oil, 14⅜" x 20". Collection Victor D. Spark, New York.

[31]
Crossing the Ford—Platte River, Colorado, oil, 40" x 68". Collection The Century Association, New York.

BLAKELOCK, RALPH ALBERT

[32]
Rocky Mountains, oil, 34¾" x 55½". Collection Berkshire Museum, Pittsfield, Massachusetts.

MEEKER, JOSEPH RUSLING

[33]
In the Swamp Opposite Bayou Sara, oil, 19½" x 20". Collection Edward Eberstadt and Sons, New York.

STIEFFEL, HERMANN

[34]
The Wichita Mountains from the Medicine Bluffs, watercolor, 16¾" x 23½". Collection Smithsonian Institution, Washington.

[35]
The Yellowstone River near Fort Keough, Montana, watercolor, 13⅝" x 22". Collection Smithsonian Institution, Washington.

MORAN, THOMAS

[36]
Hot Springs near the Yellowstone, gouache,
9" x 14". Collection Edward Eberstadt
and Sons, New York.

[37]
Giant Blue Spring, Yellowstone Region,
pastel, 10" x 14". Collection M. Knoedler
and Company, New York.

[38]
*Cliffs of the Green River, Wyoming Terri-
tory*, oil, 26½" x 34¼". Collection Smithsonian Institution, Washington.

THE INDIAN

SAINT-MEMIN, CHARLES BALTHA-
ZAR JULIEN FEVRET DE

[39]
Mandan Woman, watercolor, 7¼" x 6½".
Collection Kennedy Galleries, Inc., New
York.

[40]
Mandan Man, watercolor, 7¼" x 6½".
Collection Kennedy Galleries, Inc., New
York.

SEYMOUR, SAMUEL

[41]
Pawnee Council, watercolor, 8½" x 10⅝".
Collection William Robertson Coe, Yale
University Library.

[42]
Dog Dance of the Kansas Indians, water-
color, 8½" x 10⅝". Collection William
Robertson Coe, Yale University Library.

KING, CHARLES BIRD

[43]
*Young Omahaw, War Eagle, Little Mis-
souri and Pawnees*, oil, 27¾" x 35¾".
Collection Smithsonian Institution, Washington.

[44]
Shaumonekusse, Chief of the Otoes, oil, 30"
x 25". Collection M. Knoedler and Company, New York.

[45]
"No Heart" — Ioway, oil, 17⅜" x 13¼".
Collection Smithsonian Institution. Wash-
ington.

RINDISBACHER, PETER

[46]
Inside of an Indian Tent, watercolor, 8⅜"
x 10¼". Collection Peabody Museum, Harvard University.

[47]
Indians Returning from War, watercolor,
10¼" x 8¼". Collection Peabody Museum,
Harvard University.

[48]
Buffalo Hunting in Summer, watercolor,
9⅜" x 17⅛". Collection Peabody Museum,
Harvard University.

[49]
Indians Hunting Buffalo, tempera on
paper, 17⅛" x 30". Collection Ernest R.
Reiff, North St. Paul.

[50]
War Dance of the Sauks and Foxes, watercolor, 12" x 18". Collection Schloss Neuwied, Germany. Courtesy Prinz Dietrich
zu Wied.

[51]
Indian Dance, watercolor, 12" x 18". Collection Schloss Neuwied, Germany. Courtesy Prinz Dietrich zu Wied.

CATLIN, GEORGE

[52]
"Black Hawk", oil, 28" x 23". Collection
Smithsonian Institution, Washington.

[53]
*View on the Upper Missouri River—Ric-
caree Village*, oil, 11" x 14¼". Collection
Smithsonian Institution, Washington.

[54]
Buffalo Chase, oil, 18" x 24½". Collection
American Museum of Natural History, New
York.

[55]
Buffalo Hunt, Under the Wolf Mask, oil,
18¾" x 26". Collection Smithsonian Institution, Washington.

[56]
Scalp Dance, oil, 18¾" x 26". Collection
Smithsonian Institution, Washington.

[57]
Snow-shoe Dance of the Ojibbeway, oil, 18¾" x 26". Collection Smithsonian Institution, Washington.

[58]
"The Blue Medicine", oil, 28" x 23". Collection Smithsonian Institution, Washington.

[59]
"He who Drinks the Juice of the Stone", oil, 28" x 23". Collection Smithsonian Institution, Washington.

[60]
"Sam Perryman", oil, 28" x 23". Collection Smithsonian Institution, Washington.

BODMER, CHARLES

[61]
Indian Pipe Smoker, watercolor, 10" x 12½". Collection Schloss Neuwied, Germany. Courtesy Prinz Dietrich zu Wied.

[62]
Choctaw Indian in Blanket with Powder Horn and Pouch, watercolor, 8¾" x 6⅜". Collection Schloss Neuwied, Germany. Courtesy Prinz Dietrich zu Wied.

[63]
Choctaw Indian in White Man's Shirt and Blue Waistcoat, watercolor, 8¾" x 6⅜". Collection Schloss Neuwied, Germany. Courtesy Prinz Dietrich zu Wied.

[64]
Choctaw Indian in White Man's Ruffled Shirt, watercolor, 8¾" x 6⅜". Collection Schloss Neuwied, Germany. Courtesy Prinz Dietrich zu Wied.

[65]
Winter Village of the Minitarees, colored aquatint, 22" x 25½". Collection James Jerome Hill Reference Library, St. Paul.

[66]
Minitaree Warrior in Costume of the Dog Dance, colored aquatint, 28" x 21". Collection James Jerome Hill Reference Library, St. Paul.

[67]
The Interior of the Hut of a Mandan Chief, colored aquatint, 22" x 25½". Collection James Jerome Hill Reference Library, St. Paul.

[68]
Tombs of Assiniboin Indians, colored aquatint, 28" x 21". Collection James Jerome Hill Reference Library, St. Paul.

MILLER, ALFRED JACOB

[69]
Indian Pursuit, oil, 14" x 20". Collection Everett D. Graff, Chicago.

[70]
The Surround, oil, 66¼" x 94½". Collection M. Knoedler and Company, New York.

EASTMAN, SETH

[71]
Wenona's Leap, watercolor, 13⅛" x 16⅛". Collection James Jerome Hill Reference Library, St. Paul.

[72]
Lacrosse Playing Among the Sioux Indians, oil, 28" x 40". Collection Corcoran Gallery of Art, Washington.

[73]
Indian Sugar Camp, watercolor, 13⅛" x 16⅛". Collection James Jerome Hill Reference Library, St. Paul.

[74]
Indians Travelling, watercolor, 13⅛" x 16⅛". Collection James Jerome Hill Reference Library, St. Paul.

[75]
Dacota Encampment, watercolor, 13⅛" x 16⅛". Collection James Jerome Hill Reference Library, St. Paul.

[76]
Dacota Village, watercolor, 13⅛" x 16⅛". Collection James Jerome Hill Reference Library, St. Paul.

STANLEY, JOHN MIX

[77]
An Osage Scalp Dance, oil, 40" x 60". Collection Smithsonian Institution, Washington.

[78]
Prairie Indian Encampment, oil, 9⅛" x 14⅛". Collection The Detroit Institute of Arts.

[79]
Chinook Burial Grounds, oil, 9⅛″ x 14⅛″. Collection The Detroit Institute of Arts.

[80]
Indian Telegraph, oil, 20″ x 15½″. Collection The Detroit Institute of Arts.

[81]
Assiniboin Encampment on the Upper Missouri, oil, 7½″ x 9½″. Collection The Detroit Institute of Arts.

BINGHAM, GEORGE CALEB

[82]
The Concealed Enemy, oil, 29″ x 36″. Collection Peabody Museum, Harvard University.

WIMAR, CHARLES

[83]
Indian Camp Fire, oil, 15″ x 27″. Collection Robert B. Honeyman, Jr., Pasadena.

[84]
The Captive Charger, oil, 30″ x 41″. Collection City Art Museum of St. Louis. Gift of Miss Lillie B. Randall.

[85]
Medicine Bag, oil, 12⅜″ x 9″. Collection City Art Museum of St. Louis.

[86]
Indians Approaching Fort Benton, oil, 23″ x 47″. Collection Washington University, St. Louis.

[87]
The Buffalo Hunt, oil, 36″ x 60″. Collection Washington University, St. Louis.

[88]
The Buffalo Dance, oil, 24⅞″ x 49⅝″. Collection City Art Museum of St. Louis. Gift of Mrs. John T. Davis.

BIERSTADT, ALBERT

[89]
The Last of the Buffalo, oil, 69″ x 117″. Collection Corcoran Gallery of Art, Washington.

BUCHSER, FRANK

[90]
Indian Camp at Fort Laramie, oil, 13½″ x 15⅜″. Collection Kunstmuseum, Basel, Switzerland.

STIEFFEL, HERMANN

[91]
Sa-tan-ti Addressing the Peace Commissioners at Council Grove, Medicine Lodge Creek, 1867, watercolor, 15″ x 22″. Collection Smithsonian Institution, Washington.

FRENZENY, PAUL

[92]
The Ambush, oil, 42″ x 30″. Collection Edward Eberstadt and Sons, New York.

REMINGTON, FREDERIC

[93]
The Scout: Friends or Enemies, oil, 27″ x 40″. Private collection.

THE BIRDS AND ANIMALS

AUDUBON, JOHN JAMES

[94]
Green Heron, watercolor, 17¾″ x 22¾″. Collection Harvard College Library.

[95]
Ivory-billed Woodpecker, watercolor, 27⅞″ x 21¾″. Collection Harvard College Library.

[96]
Red-tailed Hawk, watercolor, 27⅞″ x 21⅞″. Collection Harvard College Library.

[97]
Wild Turkey Cock, colored engraving, 38½″ x 25⅜″. Collection City Art Museum of St. Louis.

[98]
Whooping Crane, colored engraving, 25¾″ x 38¾″. Collection Kennedy Galleries, Inc., New York.

[99]
Barn Owl, colored engraving, 33⅞" x 22⅞". Collection City Art Museum of St. Louis.

[100]
Turkey Buzzard, colored engraving, 37¾" x 24¾". Collection Mercantile Library, St. Louis.

[101]
Pinnated Grouse or Prairie Chicken, colored engraving, 37¾" x 24¾". Collection Mercantile Library, St. Louis.

[102]
Cock of the Plains or Sage Grouse, colored engraving, 37¾" x 24¾". Collection Mercantile Library, St. Louis.

[103]
Carolina Parrot or Parakeet, colored engraving, 33" x 22". Collection Old Print Shop, New York.

RINDISBACHER, PETER

[104]
Buffaloes in Winter, watercolor, 9½" x 17". Collection Peabody Museum, Harvard University.

BODMER, CHARLES

[105]
Head of a Bighorn Calf, watercolor, 10⅝" x 13¼". Collection Schloss Neuwied, Germany. Courtesy Prinz Dietrich zu Wied.

[106]
Head of a Prong-horned Antelope Calf, watercolor, 9⅝" x 11¼". Collection Schloss Neuwied, Germany. Courtesy Prinz Dietrich zu Wied.

[107]
Beaver Hut on the Missouri, colored aquatint, 12½" x 17⅝". Collection James Jerome Hill Reference Library, St. Paul.

MILLER, ALFRED JACOB

[108]
Scenting the Breeze, watercolor, 16" x 16½". Collection Mrs. Clyde H. Porter, Kansas City.

[109]
Buffaloes Drinking and Bathing at Night, watercolor, 7½" x 12". Collection Mrs. Clyde H. Porter, Kansas City.

AUDUBON, JOHN JAMES

[110]
Black-tailed Hare or Jack Rabbit, watercolor, 15¾" x 22¾". Collection City Art Museum of St. Louis.

[111]
Fisher or Marten, watercolor, 18" x 30". Collection Henry Schnakenberg, Newton, Connecticut.

[112]
Wolverene, watercolor, 32¾" x 43½". Collection American Museum of Natural History, New York.

[113]
Say's or Western Fox Squirrel, watercolor, 18¾" x 24⅞". Collection The Boatmen's National Bank of St. Louis.

[114]
Head of a Buffalo Calf, watercolor, 24" x 30". Collection Frank H. Shaffer, Jr., Cincinnati.

[115]
Leopard Ground-Squirrel or Chipmunk, colored lithograph, 22" x 28". Collection Mr. and Mrs. Edwin Grossman, St. Louis.

[116]
Prairie Dogs, colored lithograph, 21" x 27¼". Collection Mr. and Mrs. Edwin Grossman, St. Louis.

AUDUBON, JOHN WOODHOUSE

[117]
Prong-horned Antelope, oil, 26¼" x 32¼". Collection American Museum of Natural History, New York.

[118]
Common American Deer, oil, 32¼" x 38½". Collection American Museum of Natural History, New York.

AUDUBON, JOHN JAMES

[119]
Black-tailed Deer, colored lithograph, 20¾" x 27½". Collection Mr. and Mrs. Edwin Grossman, St. Louis.

AUDUBON, JOHN WOODHOUSE

[120]
Prairie Wolf or Coyote, oil, 24¼" x 28¾".
Collection American Museum of Natural
History, New York.

[121]
Gray Wolf or White American Wolf, oil,
27" x 32½". Collection American Museum
of Natural History, New York.

[122]
Grizzly Bear, colored lithograph, 21" x 27".
Collection Mr. and Mrs. Edwin Grossman,
St. Louis.

RANNEY, WILLIAM T.

[123]
The Lasso, oil, 36" x 54½". Collection M.
Knoedler and Company, New York.

WIMAR, CHARLES

[124]
Buffaloes Crossing the Yellowstone, oil,
24" x 48". Collection Washington University, St. Louis.

[125]
Studies of a Quartered Buffalo, oil, 8" x
11⅝". Collection City Art Museum of
St. Louis.

BIERSTADT, ALBERT

[126]
Buffalo Bull, oil, 14" x 19". Collection
Newark Museum, Newark, New Jersey.

[127]
Thunderstorm in the Rocky Mountains, oil,
19" x 29". Collection Museum of Fine
Arts, Boston.

HAYS, WILLIAM JACOB

[128]
Wapiti, oil, 26" x 48". Collection Edward
Eberstadt and Sons, New York.

BUCHSER, FRANK

[129]
Cadaver of an Ox, oil, . . . x . . . Collection Kunstmuseum, Basel, Switzerland.

THE WHITE MAN

SAINT-AULAIRE, FELIX ACHILLE

[130]
Keelboat on the Mississippi, colored litho-
graph, 11¾" x 17⅛". Collection City
Art Museum of St. Louis.

VON PHUL, ANNA MARIA

[131]
Two Young Ladies, watercolor, 7⅛" x 9".
Collection Missouri Historical Society, St.
Louis.

[132]
Boy in Beaver Hat, watercolor, 10" x 7¾".
Collection Missouri Historical Society, St.
Louis.

[133]
Young Gentleman of Fashion, watercolor,
10" x 7¾". Collection Missouri Historical
Society, St. Louis.

[134]
St. Louis Belle, watercolor, 8¾" x 6¾".
Collection Missouri Historical Society, St.
Louis.

MILLER, ALFRED JACOB

[135]
Bull-boating, watercolor, 8¾" x 15¼".
Collection Mrs. Clyde H. Porter, Kansas
City.

[136]
Prairie on Fire, watercolor, 8¾" x 14½".
Collection Mrs. Clyde H. Porter, Kansas
City.

[137]
Rendezvous in the Wind River Mountains,
oil, 26" x 38". Collection Everett D. Graff,
Chicago.

[138]
*Sir William Drummond Stewart's Caravan
on the Platte*, oil, 26" x 52¼". The Boatmen's National Bank of St. Louis.

ABBE, MRS. S. B.

[139]
The Voyageur, oil, 10¾" x 8⅝". Collection Minnesota Historical Society, St. Paul.

DEAS, CHARLES

[140]
The Trapper or Long Jakes, oil, 33½″ x 26″. Courtesy Mabel Brady Garvan. Collection Yale University Art Gallery.

EASTMAN, SETH

[141]
Emigrants Attacked by the Comanches, watercolor, 13⅛″ x 16⅛″. Collection James Jerome Hill Reference Library, St. Paul.

RANNEY, WILLIAM T.

[142]
The Prairie Fire, oil, 38″ x 60″. Collection Claude J. Ranney, Malvern, Pennsylvania.

[143]
Prairie Burial, oil, 28½″ x 41″. Collection Mr. and Mrs. J. Maxwell Moran, Malvern, Pennsylvania.

[144]
The Pioneers, oil, 24″ x 36″. Collection Claude J. Ranney, Malvern, Pennsylvania.

[145]
Caravan on the Prairies, oil, 8″ x 14½″. Collection Mr. and Mrs. John F. Merriam, Omaha.

[146]
The Trappers, oil, 23″ x 36″. Collection M. Knoedler and Company, New York.

[147]
The Retreat, oil, 30½″ x 48½″. Collection M. Knoedler and Company, New York.

[148]
The Scouting Party, oil, 30″ x 40″. Collection Claude J. Ranney, Malvern, Pennsylvania.

BALDWIN, WILLIAM

[149]
The Merry Raftsmen, oil, 21″ x 30⅜″. Collection City Art Museum of St. Louis.

BINGHAM, GEORGE CALEB

[150]
The Jolly Flatboatmen, oil, 38″ x 48½″. Collection Claiborne Pell, Washington.

[151]
Negro Boy, drawing, 12″ x 8¼″. Collection Mercantile Library, St. Louis.

[152]
Bull-Whacker, drawing, 12¾″ x 7″. Collection Mercantile Library, St. Louis.

[153]
Respected Citizen, drawing, 9¾″ x 11½″. Collection Mercantile Library, St. Louis.

[154]
Man Listening to a Speech, drawing, 12½″ x 9¾″. Collection Mercantile Library, St. Louis.

[155]
Farm Hand, drawing, 11″ x 9½″. Collection Mercantile Library, St. Louis.

[156]
Wayfarer, drawing, 9¾″ x 8¼″. Collection Mercantile Library, St. Louis.

[157]
Shooting for the Beef, oil, 33½″ x 49¼″. Collection The Brooklyn Museum. Presented in memory of Dick S. Ramsay.

[158]
The Wood-Boat, oil, 24¾″ x 29⅝″. Collection City Art Museum of St. Louis.

[159]
The County Election, oil, 49″ x 63″. Collection The Boatmen's National Bank of St. Louis.

[160]
Stump Speaking, oil, 42½″ x 58″. Collection The Boatmen's National Bank of St. Louis.

[161]
The Verdict of the People, oil, 46″ x 65″. Collection The Boatmen's National Bank of St. Louis.

[162]
Captured by Indians, oil, 25″ x 30″. Collection Arthur Hoskins, St. Louis.

[163]
The Belated Wayfarers, oil, 25″ x 30″. Collection Arthur Hoskins, St. Louis.

WIMAR, CHARLES

[164]

Attack on an Emigrant Train, pencil and charcoal, 32⅞" x 48⅛". Collection City Art Museum of St. Louis.

[165]

Attack on an Emigrant Train, drawing, 36¾" x 49¼". Collection City Art Museum of St. Louis.

[166]

Turf House on the Plains, oil, 6" x 12". Collection Robert B. Honeyman, Jr., Pasadena.

TAIT, ARTHUR FITZ WILLIAM

[167]

American Frontier Life, oil, 24⅜" x 26¼". Collection Yale University Art Gallery. Whitney Collections of Sporting Art.

PALMER, FRANCES F.

[168]

The Rocky Mountains. Emigrants Crossing the Plains, colored lithograph, 22⅛" x 30". Collection Chicago Historical Society.

TAIT, ARTHUR FITZ WILLIAM

[169]

Trappers at Fault Looking for the Trail, oil, 36" x 50". Collection M. Knoedler and Company, New York.

BIERSTADT, ALBERT

[170]

Nooning on the Platte, oil, 6¾" x 12⅞". Collection City Art Museum of St. Louis.

[171]

Surveyor's Wagon in the Rockies, oil, 7¾" x 12⅞". Collection City Art Museum of St. Louis.

[172]

The Oregon Trail, oil, 31" x 49". Collection The Butler Institute of American Art, Youngstown, Ohio.

BUCHSER, FRANK

[173]

Ford on the Platte, oil, 13¾" x 26⅝". Collection Kunstmuseum, Basel, Switzerland.

[174]

Tent Encampment at Night, oil, 14¼" x 35½". Collection Kunstverein, Solothurn, Switzerland.

[175]

Sunrise: Laramie Plains, oil, 36¼" x 57⅞". Collection Kunstmuseum, Basel, Switzerland.

[176]

Consultation, drawing. . . . x . . . Collection Kunstmuseum, Basel, Switzerland.

[177]

The Last Moment in Virginia Dale, drawing. . . . x . . . Collection Kunstmuseum, Basel, Switzerland.

[178]

Return from Idaho to Virginia Dale, drawing. . . . x . . . Collection Kunstmuseum, Basel, Switzerland.

COLMAN, SAMUEL

[179]

Covered Wagons Crossing Medicine Bow Creek, oil, 19" x 33". Collection Hall Park McCullough, North Bennington, Vermont.

[180]

Ships of the Plains, oil, 49" x 97". Collection The Union League Club, New York.

EAKINS, THOMAS

[181]

Cowboys in the Bad Lands, oil, 39" x 52". Collection Mrs. Francis P. Garvan, Roslyn, New York.

THE SETTLEMENTS: FORTS, TOWNS AND CITIES

VON PHUL, ANNA MARIA

[182]
A Creole Farm near St. Louis, wash drawing, 7⅞" x 9⅞". Collection Missouri Historical Society, St. Louis.

[183]
A Corner of St. Louis by the River, wash drawing, 6¼" x 8". Collection Missouri Historical Society, St. Louis.

MILLER, ALFRED JACOB

[184]
Fort Laramie, watercolor, 6½" x 9½". Collection Mrs. Clyde H. Porter, Kansas City.

[185]
Interior of Fort Laramie, watercolor, 11⅝" x 14⅛". Collection Walters Art Gallery, Baltimore.

BODMER, CHARLES

[186]
Fort Clark, colored aquatint, 22" x 25½". Collection James Jerome Hill Reference Library, St. Paul.

[187]
Fort Pierre, colored aquatint, 22" x 25½". Collection James Jerome Hill Reference Library, St. Paul.

WILD, JOHN CASPER

[188]
View of St. Louis, colored lithograph, 20½" x 27⅝". Collection Chicago Historical Society.

[189]
Fort Snelling, watercolor and gouache, 19" x 30". Collection Minnesota Historical Society, St. Paul.

UNKNOWN ARTIST

[190]
St. Charles, Missouri, colored lithograph, 17" x 27½". Collection Kennedy Galleries, Inc., New York.

[191]
Independence—Court House, Missouri, engraving, 7¼" x 10¾". Collection Missouri Historical Society, St. Louis.

[192]
Weston, Missouri, pencil drawing, 5¾" x 7⅛". Collection City Art Museum of St. Louis.

LEWIS, HENRY

[193]
Carondelet, Missouri, colored lithograph, 7¼" x 10¾". Collection City Art Museum of St. Louis.

UNKNOWN ARTIST

[194]
View of St. Louis from Lucas Place, colored lithograph, 24⅛" x 38". Collection Chicago Historical Society.

ROBYN, EDUARD

[195]
Washington, Missouri, colored lithograph, 21¼" x 26¼". Collection Missouri Historical Society, St. Louis.

[196]
Hermann, Missouri, colored lithograph, 21" x 27". Collection Missouri Historical Society, St. Louis.

HILL, JOHN WILLIAM

[197]
New Orleans from St. Patrick's Church, colored lithograph, 29½" x 44½". Collection Chicago Historical Society.

BOURNE, WILLIAM

[198]
City of Burlington, Iowa, colored lithograph, 18½" x 26½". Collection Kennedy Galleries, Inc., New York.

WRIGHT, RUFUS

[199]
City of Davenport, Iowa, colored lithograph, 19¾" x 27⅜". Collection Chicago Historical Society.

REYNOLDS, G. L.

[200]
Des Moines, Iowa, From the Capitol, colored lithograph, 23" x 38½". Collection Kennedy Galleries, Inc., New York.

HAKLHUBER, F.

[201]
Herndon Hotel, Omaha, Nebraska, watercolor, 9½" x 12⅝". Collection Missouri Historical Society, St. Louis.

KURZ, LEWIS

[202]
Omaha, Nebraska, colored lithograph, 21¾" x 28". Collection Chicago Historical Society.

LEUTZE, EMANUEL

[203]
Gulch Mine, Central City, Colorado, watercolor, 15" x 20". Collection Denver Public Library.

MATHEWS, ALFRED E.

[204]
Pike's Peak and Colorado City, colored lithograph, 13¼" x 17⅝". Collection Chicago Historical Society.

COLYER, VINCENT

[205]
Fort Arbuckle, Oklahoma Territory, watercolor, 6" x 10½". Collection Edward Eberstadt and Sons, New York.

UNKNOWN ARTIST

[206]
The Bridge at St. Louis, colored lithograph, 27¾" x 38½". Collection Library of Congress.

ELLSBURY, GEORGE H.

[207]
St. Paul, Minnesota, colored lithograph, 20¼" x 32⅝". Collection Chicago Historical Society.

RUGER, A.

[208]
Minneapolis, Minnesota, lithograph, 23" x 36". Collection Chicago Historical Society.

ELLSBURY, GEORGE H. AND
GREEN, VERNON

[209]
Winona, Minnesota, colored lithograph, 16⅛" x 28⅛". Collection Kennedy Galleries, Inc., New York.

RICHARDS, GEORGE I.

[210]
Red Wing, Minnesota, colored lithograph, 18" x 29⅞". Collection Chicago Historical Society.

STIEFFEL, HERMANN

[211]
Fort Harker, Kansas, watercolor, 13¾" x 21¾". Collection Smithsonian Institution, Washington.

[212]
Miles City, Montana, watercolor, 17½" x 25½". Collection Smithsonian Institution, Washington.

[213]
Fort Keough, Montana, watercolor, 17½" x 25½". Collection Smithsonian Institution, Washington.

WESTWARD BY LAND AND BY WATER

BODMER, CHARLES

[214]
Steamer "Yellowstone," colored aquatint, 22" x 25½". Collection James Jerome Hill Reference Library, St. Paul.

UNKNOWN ARTIST

[215]
Steamboat Loading Passengers, watercolor, 7⅝" x 13⅞". Collection City Art Museum of St. Louis.

PARSONS, C. H.

[216]
High Pressure Steamboat Mayflower, colored lithograph, 16⅜" x 28⅛". Collection City Art Museum of St. Louis.

PALMER, FRANCES F.

[217]
Steamboats on the Mississippi, drawing, 18" x 27". Collection Victor D. Spark, New York.

FULLER, GEORGE F.

[218]
Bound Down the River, colored lithograph, 22" x 29½". Collection City Art Museum of St. Louis.

OTTER, THOMAS

[219]
On the Road, oil, 22⅛" x 45⅜". Collection William Rockhill Nelson Gallery of Art, Kansas City.

PALMER, FRANCES F.

[220]
Across the Continent: Westward the Course of Empire Takes its Way, colored lithograph, 22½" x 31½". Collection Louis W. Hill, Jr., St. Paul.

THOMAS, H. AND D. DRUMMOND

[221]
Locomotive Arkansas with Tender McKay of the Little Rock and Fort Smith Railway, colored lithograph, 26¼" x 34". Collection A. Howard Stebbins, Jr., Little Rock.

CURRIER AND IVES

[222]
Prairie Fires of the Great West, colored lithograph, 10" x 14". Collection Chicago Historical Society.

STIEFFEL, HERMANN

[223]
Fort Harker, Kansas, watercolor, 17" x 23½". Collection Smithsonian Institution, Washington.

TROTTER, NEWBOLD H.

[224]
Held Up, oil, 42" x 57½". Collection Smithsonian Institution, Washington.

Biographies of the Artists

AUDUBON, JOHN JAMES
Born at Les Cayes, Santo Domingo, in 1785, natural son of a French naval officer. Reared in France and first came to the United States in 1804 and made his earliest drawings of birds. In 1806 studied drawing in Paris studio of Jacques Louis David. Returned to America and lived variously in Pennsylvania, Kentucky, Missouri and Ohio. In Cincinnati, where he was employed in Dr. Daniel Drake's natural history museum, decided on his monumental *Birds of America*. To New Orleans by Mississippi flatboat in 1820 where he painted portraits and pursued bird project. 1826-29 in London, Edinburgh, Paris arranging for publication and securing subscribers. Commenced publication of *Birds* in 1827, completed in 1838. To England again 1830-31, then traveled from Florida to Labrador in search of bird specimens. Commenced work on *Quadrupeds of North America* in 1839. Made trip up Missouri from St. Louis to Fort Union in 1843 and overland trip up the Yellowstone in search of specimens. Began publication in 1845. Died in New York in 1851.

AUDUBON, JOHN WOODHOUSE
Born in Kentucky in 1812, son and pupil of John James Audubon. Accompanied his father in travels to Florida and Labrador searching for specimens. Briefly attempted a business career in Louisville and clerked on a Mississippi steamboat. Rejoined his father in his projects in 1833. To Europe with his father in 1834 where he continued training in art. Collaborated with father on plates and text of the *Quadrupeds*. To Texas in 1845 to collect animal specimens. 1846-47 in London painting in the Zoological Gardens. In 1849 organized unsuccessful expedition to California in search of gold, as well as animal specimens. Died in New York in 1862.

BIERSTADT, ALBERT
Born at Solingen near Düsseldorf, Germany in 1830. At the age of two came to New Bedford, Mass. with his parents. Educated there. To Düsseldorf in 1853 to study at the Academy under Lessing, Achenbach, Leutze and the American, Whittredge. Traveled in Germany and Switzerland and painted in Rome for a winter with Whittredge and made a walking trip with Sandford R. Gifford through the Apennines. Returned to New Bedford in 1857. Traveled West with General F. W. Lander's surveying expedition in 1858 as far as Oregon. On a government commission to Europe in 1867. Made later trips to the West. Established a vogue for the huge and grandiloquent paintings of the mountains of the West. Decorated by the Czar of Russia, Sultan of Turkey and others. Died in New York in 1902.

BINGHAM, GEORGE CALEB
Born in Augusta Co., Virginia in 1811. Moved with family to central Missouri in 1819. Studied for the law and the ministry. Turned to painting and was self-taught. Early activity as portraitist. Active in St. Louis and Natchez 1835-36. Studied for three months at Pennsylvania Academy, Philadelphia, 1837. Painted portraits in Washington 1840-44. In 1844 upon his return to Missouri commenced his series of genre paintings with *The Jolly Flatboatmen*. In Missouri 1844-53. Active in the American Art Union. Promoted his art by engraved reproductions. Painted local political genre as well as portraits, landscapes and riverboat scenes. In Philadelphia 1853-54. To Europe in 1856; studied and painted in Düsseldorf until 1859. Returned to Missouri. Always active in state and local politics; became increasingly so. Served in Union Army 1861. Professor of art, University of Missouri, 1877. Died in Kansas City in 1879.

BLAKELOCK, RALPH ALBERT
Born in New York in 1847. Educated there and showed his talent for drawing at school.

Self-taught as painter. In 1867 exhibited a landscape at the National Academy of Design. To the Far West in 1869 and probably remained three years. Became especially interested in the Indian and the landscape of the Rockies. Made many ink drawings which became the basis of his paintings of the West. Indian theme persisted in his art after this trip, but he always saw the Indian poetically, as part of nature. His art was unappreciated and he lived in desperate poverty. Mental breakdown in 1899. Most of remainder of his life in asylums and sanitariums. Died in the Adirondacks in 1919.

BODMER, CHARLES
Born in Riesbach near Tieffenbrunnen, Switzerland in 1809. Trained as an artist by his uncle, J. J. Meyer von Meilen. In 1832-34 traveled up the Missouri to Fort McKenzie with the German naturalist, Maximilian, Prince of Wied, as his commissioned artist. Painted many watercolors of the Plains Indians, the wild life and landscape which were published as aquatints to illustrate Maximilian's book, *Journey into the Interior of North America* in 1839. Returned to Europe in 1834 and settled first in Paris and in 1849 at Barbizon where he adopted the attitude of his fellow artists there and once collaborated with J. F. Millet as an illustrator. From 1836 on he was a more or less regular exhibitor at the Paris Salon. Died at Barbizon in 1893.

BUCHSER, FRANK
Born in Feldbrunn near Solothurn, Switzerland in 1828 as Franz Buchser. Apprenticed to an organ maker as a boy. Then traveled to Paris and Italy. In 1847 decided to become a painter. Brief service in papal guards. 1850-53 spent in Paris, Belgium, Holland, Spain and England. Returned to Solothurn in 1855. In 1857 continued his wanderings in Spain and Morocco as Spanish battle painter in Moroccan campaign. 1861-63 again in England. To America in 1866 and painted numerous portraits of political figures and Negro types in Virginia. Changed his first name to Frank. Spent summer of 1866 in the West as companion of General Sherman. Made many oil studies and sketches. In 1868 spent summer on the Great Lakes. Returned to Europe 1871 and

traveled extensively during 'seventies and 'eighties in Italy, Dalmatia and Greece. Concerned himself with welfare of Swiss artists; founded Swiss Artists Association and promoted the Swiss "Salon". Died in Solothurn in 1890.

CATLIN, GEORGE
Born in Wilkes-Barre, Pa. in 1796. Studied law at Litchfield, Conn. in 1817-18. After brief practice, taught himself to paint and commenced career as a portrait miniaturist in Philadelphia. There his first sight of Plains Indians returning West from Washington inspired his monumental project to paint all the Indian tribes between the Alleghenies and the Pacific. Painted portraits in Washington, Albany, Richmond. In 1832 voyaged up the Missouri from St. Louis painting Indians of many tribes, their daily pursuits and landscapes along the way. To the Southwest in 1834. In 1835-36 visited the upper Mississippi and Great Lakes. To South Carolina in 1837-38 to paint Seminoles. During these eight years he visited forty-eight tribes and painted upwards of five hundred canvases of Indians, Indian life and wild animals. Many of them were published in his *North American Indians* in 1841. From 1837 to 1852 traveled with his "Indian Gallery" of paintings and an Indian troupe. Traveled in Central and South America 1852-57 and in Europe, 1858-70. Died in Jersey City in 1872.

COLMAN, SAMUEL
Born in Portland, Maine in 1832. At an early age moved with his family to New York where his father was a book publisher. Studied with Asher B. Durand and exhibited his first picture in 1850. Elected an associate of the National Academy of Design in 1859, and became associated with the Hudson River School. Traveled abroad in 1860-62. In 1867 was one of the founders of the American Watercolor Society. To Europe again in 1871-1875. Lived at Irvington-on-Hudson and later at Newport, R.I. Developed a forceful style with thick impasto. Specialized in the picturesque landscape of Europe and America. Died in New York in 1920.

COLYER, VINCENT
Born in 1825. Studied in New York with

John R. Smith. Elected associate of the National Academy of Design in 1849. After service in the Civil War was appointed a special United States Indian Commissioner. Active until early 'seventies traveling extensively in Southwest. Made many sketches, drawings and watercolors, especially of Army posts in the Indian territory. Died in 1888.

DEAS, CHARLES

Born in Philadelphia in 1818, the maternal grandson of Ralph Izard, Revolutionary diplomat and Senator from South Carolina. Influenced in boyhood by copies of paintings at home, by visits to the Pennsylvania Academy and Sully's studio. Failing to obtain appointment to West Point, studied art at the National Academy of Design. Inspired by a visit to Catlin's gallery of Indian Paintings, went West to join his brother at Fort Crawford, Wisconsin in 1840. From there made trips to Iowa, Fort Winnebago and Fort Snelling. Settled in St. Louis in 1841. Accompanied Major Wharton's military expedition from Fort Leavenworth to the upper Platte River in 1844. Frequently exhibited at the National Academy of Design and the American Art Union, New York during the eighteen forties. Lost his mind and for many years lived in an asylum until his death in 1867.

EAKINS, THOMAS

Born in Philadelphia in 1844, son of a writing master. Studied at the Pennsylvania Academy of the Fine Arts and took courses in anatomy at Jefferson Medical College. To Europe in 1866 and studied under Gérome at Ecole des Beaux Arts, Paris. Also studied with Bonnat. Travelled to Spain and was strongly impressed by realism of Velasquez and Ribera. Stayed in Seville. Returned to America and settled in Philadelphia in 1870. Spent summer of 1887 in South Dakota. Specialized in portraits and sporting subjects. Taught at Pennsylvania Academy. Died in Philadelphia in 1916.

EASTMAN, SETH

Born in Brunswick, Maine, in 1808. Appointed to West Point in 1824, he graduated from the Military Academy in 1829. Learned to sketch as part of his officer training. Assigned to duty at Fort Craw-

ford near Prairie du Chien, Wisconsin, then to Fort Snelling in Minnesota. Made trips West from there. Taught drawing at West Point 1833-40. Second duty at Fort Snelling 1841-48 during which he painted many Indian subjects of the tribes of Minnesota. Returned to Washington. Prepared illustrations for his wife's books on the Indians and Henry M. Schoolcraft's famous work in six volumes commissioned by Congress, *Indian Tribes of the United States*. Active duty during Civil War. In 1867 was retired from the Army as brevet brigadier general. Until his death, active painting Indian subjects commissioned by Congress. Died in Washington in 1875.

FRENZENY, PAUL

Born in France. Served in French army and had several years of duty in Mexico before 1868. Became well known as illustrator and partner of fellow Frenchman, Jules Tavernier. Together toured the West and made series of illustrations of their trip for *Harper's Weekly* 1873-74. Remained in San Francisco until 1878. Probably returned to New York in 1879 and continued to make illustrations for *Harper's* and *Leslie's Weekly* until 1889. Nothing further is known of his life.

HAYS, WILLIAM JACOB

The grandson of Jacob Hays, famous high constable of New York. Born in New York in 1830, he studied with John R. Smith. Began to exhibit at the National Academy in 1850, was elected an associate in 1852 and soon established a reputation as an animal painter. Made riverboat trip up the Missouri in 1860 beyond Fort Union to Fort Stewart. Made numerous sketches of the up-river forts and the wild animals of the Plains. The latter served as basis for his paintings of Western animals, famous in his day. Went to Nova Scotia and repeatedly to the Adirondacks to make studies of wild life. Also noted for his paintings of flowers. Died in New York in 1875.

HILL, JOHN WILLIAM

Born in England in 1812. Trained as aquatint printer and lithographer. Migrated to America. Later worked in watercolor and became known for landscapes in this medium. Also designed lithographs. Died in the United States in 1879.

KING, CHARLES BIRD

Born in Newport, R. I. in 1785. Studied as a boy with Samuel King of Newport and later with Edward Savage in New York. From 1805-12 studied with Benjamin West in London. Settled first in Philadelphia. Moved to Washington, D. C. where he settled permanently. Established himself as portrait painter. Encouraged to paint visiting Indian chiefs by Thomas L. McKenney, U. S. Superintendent of Indian Trade. By 1837 had painted eighty-nine Indian portraits, the so-called "Indian Gallery." All but three destroyed in Smithsonian Institution fire in 1865. First artist, after Saint-Memin, to paint portraits of Plains Indians. Died in Washington, D. C. in 1862.

KURZ, LEWIS

Born in Austria, in 1834. To America in 1848. Fought in the Union forces in the Civil War and was a friend of Lincoln. Made sketches of scenes in the War. Became a mural painter. Settled in Chicago and was a founder of the Art Institute. Died in Chicago in 1921.

LEWIS, HENRY

Born in Scarborough, Kent, England in 1819. To America in 1836 with two brothers. Followed trade of mechanic and carpenter. Settled in St. Louis. Self-taught as artist while employed as stage carpenter at the St. Louis Theatre. Possibly first artist to conceive idea of a moving panorama of the Mississippi. Boated entire length of the river in three summers, 1846-48 making preparatory sketches. Later used in making lithographic plates for his *Das Illustrirte Mississippithal*, published in Düsseldorf in 1854-58. After American successes with panorama, took it to England and the Continent. Settled in Düsseldorf, Germany in 1851. Became American consul there. Died in Düsseldorf in 1904.

LEUTZE, EMANUEL

Born at Gmünd, Württemberg, Germany in 1816. To Philadelphia with his family as a boy. Studied there with John A. Smith. To Düsseldorf 1841-42 and studied under Lessing. Continued studies in Munich and

Italy until 1845. Returned to Düsseldorf and was active there from 1845-59. Visited the United States in 1851 and in 1859 on a commission for the Capitol in Washington which remained unfinished. Settled in Washington in 1863 and died there in 1868.

MATHEWS, ALFRED E.

Born in Bristol, England in 1831. Migrated to America with family at age of two. Settled in Rochester, Ohio. Worked as typesetter and itinerant bookseller. Self-taught as artist and at twenty-five was selling his own drawings. Taught in a rural school in Alabama. Enlisted in Union Army in 1861 and made drawings of battles and Army life. Afterwards painted a panorama of the battles of the deep South. To Nebraska in 1865 and made sketches for lithographic prints of Nebraska City. Settled in Denver the same year and commenced his series of drawings of Colorado and Montana towns and scenery which he lithographed and published in book form. Prepared and exhibited a second moving panorama of Rocky Mountain scenery. Died near Longmont, Colorado in 1874.

MEEKER, JAMES RUSLING

Born in Newark, N. J. in 1827. Studied at the National Academy of Design, New York. Developed his landscape style from studying the paintings of Asher B. Durand. Later studied portraiture with Charles Loring Elliott. To Louisville, Ky. in 1852. Remained there five years. Settled in St. Louis in 1859. Service in Civil War as paymaster in the Union Navy. Duty in Louisiana where landscape of the bayous impressed him deeply and remained a constant subject of his art. After Civil War, active in St. Louis and Wisconsin. Died in St. Louis in 1887.

MILLER, ALFRED JACOB

Born in Baltimore in 1810. Studied with Sully in Baltimore, 1831-32. To Paris in 1833 and studied at the Ecole des Beaux Arts. The following year traveled in Italy sojourning at Rome. Active in Baltimore 1834-37. To New Orleans in 1837 where he set himself up as portrait painter. There met Capt. William Drummond Stewart, the Scottish sportsman who engaged him as artist of his expedition to the Rockies that year. Remained in West six months. 1840 at

Stewart's Scottish seat, Murthly Castle, painting in oil from watercolor sketches of the West. In London 1841. Returned to Baltimore 1842 and continued to paint Western subjects based on his sketch books, and portraits. Died in 1874.

MORAN, THOMAS
Born in Bolton, Lancashire, England in 1837. Joined his family in Philadelphia in 1844. Apprenticed to a wood engraver at eighteen; commenced to paint in watercolor. To Europe in 1862 where he came under influence of Turner in England, and on a later visit studied the masters of classical landscape on the continent, especially Claude Lorraine. In 1871 accompanied exploring expeditions of the United States Geological Survey in the Yellowstone region. His immense canvas of *The Grand Canyon of the Yellowstone* was the result of the trip and was purchased by Congress. 1873 to the Southwest with Geological Survey and painted *The Grand Canyon of the Colorado*. Repeated visits to the Far West. Devoted most of his energies to painting the mountains of the West. Active also as an etcher and illustrator. Settled in East Hampton, Long Island. Died in Santa Barbara, California in 1926.

OTTER, THOMAS
Lived in Philadelphia. Known only by his painting *Moonlight*, dated 1860, in the Wilstach Collection, Philadelphia Museum, and *On the Road*, included here.

PALMER, FRANCES FLORA
Born in Leicester, England as Frances Flora Bond in 1812. To America with her husband Edward S. Palmer in early 'forties. Accompanied by her brother and sister, Robert and Maria Bond, who were also artists as well as musicians. Settled in New York. Commenced working as artist and colorist for N. Currier, lithographer in the 'forties. May have been assisted by her brother and sister. Specialized in landscapes, railroad, Mississippi and sporting subjects. One of Currier and Ives' best known artists. Remained with the firm until her death in New York in 1876.

RANNEY, WILLIAM T.
Born at Middletown, Connecticut in 1813.

As a boy apprenticed to a tinsmith in North Carolina. In 1833 received instruction in drawing in Brooklyn. Active in New York as a portrait painter 1843-46. Enlisted in the Army at the outbreak of the Mexican War, went to the Southwest and was assigned to duty in Texas. The Plains life he observed at this time influenced his art for the remainder of his life. Returned to New York. Elected an associate of the National Academy of Design in 1850. Settled in West Hoboken, New Jersey where he died in 1857. Uncompleted canvases in his studio were finished by W. S. Mount.

REMINGTON, FREDERIC
Born in Canton, N. Y. in 1861. Grew up there and in Ogdensburg, N. Y. on the St. Lawrence. Showed ability at drawing as a boy. Attended Yale and studied art there. Impressed by paintings by Detaille and de Neuville. To the West in 1880 and worked as cowboy and prospector. Settled in Kansas. Began to draw and paint in earnest and moved to Kansas City. To New York in 1885 and commenced working as illustrator for picture magazines and book publishers, and commenced to paint. Made repeated trips to the West for subject matter. In 1895 turned to sculpture. Became best known artist of the West at the end of the nineteenth century. Died at Ridgefield, Conn. in 1909.

RINDISBACHER, PETER
Born in Upper Emmenthal, Canton of Berne, Switzerland in 1806. Accompanied his parents to America in 1821. Self-taught. With other Swiss settlers in Lord Selkirk's Red River colony, first went to Manitoba via Hudson's Bay. Upon arrival in Canada commenced to paint in watercolor taking the life of the New World as his subject. Upon abandonment of the colony in 1826 he accompanied the other settlers to Fort Snelling in Minnesota. Probably late in the same year migrated with his family to Wisconsin and then alone to St. Louis where he settled in 1829 and practiced his art until his premature death in 1834. In addition to his Indian subjects, he painted miniatures and landscapes, though none of the latter are known to exist. Made drawings of Western sporting subjects and wild life for engraved illustrations in the *Amer-*

ican Turf Register. Working in the region of the Canadian border of North Dakota and Minnesota from 1821 to 1826, he was the first artist to paint the Indian in his daily pursuits and the wild animals beyond the Mississippi in their natural habitat.

ROBYN, EDUARD

Born at Emmerich on the German-Dutch frontier in 1820 or 1822 of French Huguenot family. Name originally Robin. To St. Louis in 1848 with brothers. Established lithography shop there producing many views of St. Louis and Missouri towns, book illustrations and maps. Also a political cartoonist. In 1850 painted a panorama of the sights of Asia, preserved in Missouri Historical Society, St. Louis. In 1858 moved to Hermann, Missouri. Died there in 1862.

SAINT-AULAIRE, FELIX ACHILLE

Born at Vercelli, Piemont, France in 1801. A marine painter and lithographer, he was a pupil of Franç and Hippolyte Garnerey.

SAINT-MEMIN, CHARLES BATHAZAR JULIEN FEVRET DE

Born in Dijon, France in 1770. Attended the Paris Military School in 1784-85. Self-taught at same time as painter and portraitist. Joined French guards in 1788. To Switzerland at outbreak of the Revolution and as lieutenant joined "Army of the Princes" about 1790. Painted monochrome miniatures in free time. To Canada in 1793. Settled in New York. Made engraved views of New York. Turned to portraiture and as such was active from 1796-1810 in New York, Philadelphia, Baltimore, Annapolis, Washington, Richmond, Norfolk and Charleston. Made first portraits of Plains Indians in Washington. Returned to France in 1810. Settled in Dijon in 1812 and became curator and restorer of the museum there in 1817. Perfected means of securing accurate profile likenesses by use of the so-called "physionotrace". Died in Dijon in 1852.

SEYMOUR, SAMUEL

Born in England. Established himself as painter and engraver in Philadelphia. Active there as early as 1801. Accompanied Major Stephen H. Long's expedition up the South Platte in 1819-20. Said to have made one hundred and fifty views. Six of them appear as illustrations in Edwin James' account of the expedition published in 1823. Again accompanied Major Long on an expedition into northern Minnesota and Manitoba in 1823 and prepared the illustrations of landscapes and Indians for the published official *Narrative* of the journey. All of Seymour's known works are in watercolor. He is said to have painted landscapes and Indian subjects in oil. Nothing more is known of his life. Exhibited his paintings at Peale's Museum, Philadelphia in 1832. First artist to paint the landscape of the West, and in a restricted and perfunctory way to depict the Indian in his native home. Except for the watercolors owned by Yale University, his paintings of the West have disappeared.

STANLEY, JOHN MIX

Born in Canandaigua, New York in 1814. At the age of twenty moved to Detroit. Apparently self-taught. Began to paint portraits and landscapes in 1835. As an itinerant artist visited Fort Snelling, Galena and Chicago. In 1842 went to Fort Gibson in Oklahoma Territory, and to New Mexico. With General Kearny in his march on San Diego, 1846. Later explored Columbia River and painted Indians of the Northwest. Visited Hawaii in 1850. In 1853 with Governor Isaac Stevens on northern railway survey expedition from St. Paul. Exhibited paintings at Smithsonian Institution and tried unsuccessfully to sell them to the Government. Smithsonian fire of 1865 destroyed all but five of entire collection. Settled in Buffalo, New York, and continued to paint Indian subjects and portraits. Moved to Detroit towards the end of his life; continued to paint and died there in 1872.

STIEFFEL, HERMANN

Born in Wiesbaden, Germany in 1826. Enlisted in the United States Army in New York in 1857. Continuously with Company K of the Fifth Infantry until he was discharged for disability, May 1882. Company K was assigned to duty in Kansas and Montana during these years. Stieffel is only known by his Army record which states that his occupation was that of printer;

and further, "character excellent, not married."

TAIT, ARTHUR FITZ WILLIAM

Born at Livesey Hall, Near Liverpool, England in 1819. At age of twelve worked for a picture dealer in Manchester. Self-taught from study of casts and original work in the Royal Manchester Institution. To America in 1850. Settled in New York. Elected member of the National Academy of Design in 1858, and exhibited repeatedly in its exhibitions. Especially interested in nature and sporting subjects. Observed nature and made studies in the Adirondacks and other haunts of wild life. Visited Europe in 1874. His skillful, realistic paintings of animals, birds, the adventures of the hunter and frontiersman were lithographed and widely appreciated in his lifetime. Died at Yonkers, New York in 1905.

TROTTER, NEWBOLD HOUGH

Born in Philadelphia in 1827. Studied in Holland under W. T. van Starkenborg, cattle painter of The Hague, but largely self-taught. Devoted himself to painting animal pictures. Active in Boston and Philadelphia. Died in Atlantic City, New Jersey in 1898.

VON PHUL, ANNA MARIA

Born in Philadelphia in 1786 of parents who had migrated from the German Pfalz. Moved with family to Lexington, Ky. in 1800. Studied there with an obscure artist couple, George and Mary Beck, recently arrived from England. Encouraged by the portraitist Matthew Harris Jouett, friend and neighbor. Visited Edwardsville, Ill. and St. Louis in 1818. Returned to Lexington. Revisited St. Louis 1820. Settled in St. Louis in 1821 and died at Edwardsville, Ill. in 1823.

WHITTREDGE, WORTHINGTON

Born near Springfield, Ohio in 1820. Went to Cincinnati as a young man where he taught himself to paint. Became increasingly interested in nature and in landscape painting; active in Cincinnati, 1838-49. Thanks to the patronage of Nicholas Longworth, went to Europe in 1849 where for three years he studied with Andreas Achenbach at Düsseldorf. In 1854 he went to Rome and

remained there four years, returning to America in 1859. In 1865-66 he traveled West with General Pope on his journey of inspection. Accompanied by Sandford R. Gifford and J. F. Kensett. Active in New York for the remainder of his life. Died at Summit, New Jersey in 1910.

WILD, JOHN CASPER

Born in Zürich, Switzerland about 1806. Spent fifteen years in Paris where he apparently studied art. Settled in Philadelphia and produced his first print there in 1831. By 1835 he was living in Cincinnati where he was active as a landscape painter and lithographer. By 1838 he had returned to Philadelphia and in 1839 settled in St. Louis. Completed a series of thirty-four lithographs published in periodical form as the *Valley of the Mississippi Illustrated*. To Fort Snelling in 1844 and settled in Davenport, Iowa in 1845 where he died in 1846.

WIMAR, CHARLES

Born in Siegburg, near Bonn, Germany in 1828. To St. Louis with his parents in 1843. Studied painting with Leon Pomarede, a St. Louis painter and decorator. 1849 assisted Pomarede in painting a moving panorama of the Mississippi. To Düsseldorf 1852-56 where he painted his first important canvases of Indian themes. Returned to St. Louis. Made repeated riverboat trips up the Missouri to observe Indians, Western landscape and wild life. Notes and sketches made on these trips used in an important series of Indian paintings. Also active as a portrait painter. In 1861 decorated new dome of the old St. Louis Courthouse with murals. First murals to be painted west of the Mississippi. Died in St. Louis in 1862.

WRIGHT, RUFUS

Born in 1832. Studied at the National Academy of Design, New York. Painted portraits of statesmen of the Civil War period. Also known for his genre subjects.

WÜRTTEMBERG, FRIEDRICH PAUL WILHELM, DUKE OF

Born in Germany in 1797, Prince Paul, as he was generally known, was educated for a military career. At the age of twenty abandoned the army to devote his life to the natural sciences. In America 1822-24, the first of five trips, when he voyaged up the Missouri as guest of the American Fur Company. Journal of this trip was published in Stuttgart in 1835. The *Foreword* refers to illustrations he intended to publish separately. Settled in Mergentheim and amassed charts, tables and other by-products of his journeys, including many sketches. Like many educated gentlemen of his day, drawing was one of his accomplishments. In America during nearly the entire decade of the fifties. Made his last trip in 1857-58. Died in 1860.